the

the aftermath of war

(Situations III)

JEAN-PAUL SARTRE

TRANSLATED BY CHRIS TURNER

LONDON NEW YORK CALCUTTA

Seagull Books, 2017

© Editions GALLIMARD, Paris, new edition in 2003

English translation © Chris Turner 2008

First published in English by Seagull Books, 2008

ISBN   978 0 8574 2 447 1

British Library Cataloguing-in-Publication Data
A catalogue record for this book is available
from the British Library

Typeset by Seagull Books, Calcutta, India
Cover designed by Sunandini Banerjee, Seagull Books
Printed in the United Kingdom by
Biddles Ltd, King's Lynn

contents

PART ONE

the republic of silence

Never were we freer than under the German Occupation. We had lost all our rights, beginning with the right to speak. We were insulted to our faces every day and had to remain silent. We were deported en masse, as workers, Jews or political prisoners. Everywhere— on the walls, on the screens and in the newspapers— we came up against the vile, insipid picture of ourselves our oppressors wanted to present to us. Because of all this, we were free. Because the Nazi venom seeped into our very thoughts, every accurate thought was a triumph. Because an all-powerful police force tried to gag us, every word became precious as a declaration of principle. Because we were wanted men and women, every one of our acts was a solemn commitment. The often atrocious circumstances of our struggle made it possible, in a word, for us to live out that unbearable, heart-rending situation known as the human condition in a candid, unvarnished way. Exile, captivity and, especially, death, which in happier times we artfully conceal, became for us the perpetual objects of our concern; we learned that they were not inevitable accidents or even constant, external dangers, but must be regarded as our *lot*, our destiny, the profound source of our human reality. Every second, we lived to the full the meaning of that banal little phrase: 'Man is mortal!' And the choice each of us made of his life and being was an authentic choice, since it was made in the presence of death, since it could always have been expressed in the form: 'Better dead than . . .'. And I am not speaking here of the elite among us who were real Resistance fighters but of all the French people who, every hour of the night and day for four years, said 'No'. The very cruelty of the enemy drove us to the extremities of this condition by forcing us to ask ourselves questions we sidestep in peacetime. All those among us with any snippets of information about the Resistance—and what Frenchman was not at one point or another in that position—asked ourselves anxiously, 'If they torture me, shall I be able to hold out?' In this way, the very question of freedom was posed, and we were on the verge of the deepest knowledge human beings can have of themselves. For the secret of a human being is not his Oedipus complex or his inferiority complex. It is the very limit of his freedom, his ability to resist torture and death.

To those involved in underground activity, the conditions of their struggle afforded a new kind of experience. They did not fight openly like soldiers. They were hunted down in solitude, arrested in solitude, and it was in an abandoned, defenceless state that they resisted torture, alone and naked in the presence of clean-shaven, well-fed, smartly dressed torturers, who mocked their wretched flesh, and who, by their untroubled consciences and boundless sense of social strength, seemed fully to have right on their side. Yet, in the depths of this solitude, it was the others, all the others, they were protecting—all their Resistance comrades. A single word could have led to

5

ten, or a hundred, arrests. Is not this total responsibility in total solitude the very revelation of our liberty? This abandonment, this solitude, this enormous risk—these were the same for everyone, for leaders and men alike. For those who carried messages without knowing what was in them and for those who directed the entire Resistance effort, the punishment was the same—imprisonment, deportation and death. In no army in the world is such an equality of risk shared by footsoldier and generalissimo. And this is why the Resistance was a true democracy: for the soldier as for the commander, the same danger, the same responsibility, the same absolute freedom within discipline. Thus, in the shadows and in blood, the strongest of Republics was forged. Each of its citizens knew he had an obligation to all and that he had to rely on himself alone. Each, in the most total abandonment, fulfilled his role in history. Each, standing against the oppressors, made the effort to be himself irremediably. And by choosing himself in freedom, he chose freedom for all. This Republic without institutions, without army or police force, was something every French person had at every turn to conquer and

assert against Nazism. We are now on the threshold
of another Republic. Let us wish that this one will, in
the full light of day, retain the austere virtues of that
Republic of Silence and Night.

Lettres françaises, September 1944.

paris under the occupation

Arriving in Paris, many English people and Americans were amazed to find us less thin than they expected. They saw elegant dresses that looked brand-new, jackets which, from a distance, still seemed serviceable. Seldom did they encounter that paleness of face, that physical degradation that is, ordinarily, the mark of starvation. Solicitude, when thwarted, turns to rancour. I fear they rather bear us a grudge for not entirely conforming to the pathetic image they had formed of us in advance. Some of them, perhaps, secretly wondered whether the Occupation had been quite so terrible; whether France should not ultimately regard as a lucky break the defeat that had put it out of action and enabled it now to recover the status of a great power, without having earned it through great sacrifices. Perhaps they thought, like the *Daily Express*, that, by comparison with the British, the French had not had such a bad time of it in those four years.

It is to these people I would like to speak. I would like to explain to them that they are wrong, that the Occupation was a terrible ordeal, that it is not certain that France can recover from it and that there is not a single French person who has not on many occasions envied the fate of their British Allies. But as I begin, I can feel how very difficult my task is. I have known this same embarrassment once before. I was back from prisoner-of-war camp and being questioned about the lives of the prisoners: how was I to convey the atmosphere of the camps to people who hadn't been in them? With just a hint in one direction, all would seem doom and gloom; with a nudge in the other, all would look sweetness and light. The truth was not even 'halfway between the two'. It took a lot of inventiveness and skill to tell it, and a lot of goodwill and imagination to have it understood. I find myself faced with a similar problem today: how can I convey what Occupation was like to the residents of countries that remained free? There is an abyss between us and words cannot bridge it. When the French talk among themselves about the Germans, the Gestapo, the Resistance and the black market, they understand each other easily; but this is because they experienced the same things and they are filled with the same memories. The British and the French no longer have any shared memories; all that London lived through proudly, Paris lived out in despair and shame. We shall have to learn to speak of ourselves without passion; you will have to learn to understand our voices and grasp what, beyond words, can only be hinted at, and all that a gesture or a silence may mean.

Yet if I try to provide a glimpse of the truth, I run up against new difficulties: the Occupation of France was an immense social phenomenon concerning thirty-five million human beings. How can I speak for all of them? The little towns, the big industrial centres and the countryside met with different fates. Some villages never saw a German, while others had the occupying forces billeted on them for four years. Since I lived mainly in Paris, I shall confine myself to

describing the Occupation in Paris. I shall leave aside
the physical suffering, the hunger, which was genuine
but hidden, our depressed vitality, the increased inci-
dence of tuberculosis. After all, these woes, the extent
of which will one day be revealed by the statistics, are
not without their equivalent in Britain. Doubtless the
standard of living remained appreciably higher over
there than with us, but you had the bombing, the V1s
and the military casualties; we were not fighting at all.
But there are other ordeals. It is these I want to write
about, I want to try to show how Parisians *experienced*
the Occupation *emotionally*.

We must first rid ourselves of stereotypes: no, the
Germans were not patrolling the streets with guns in
their hands; no, they didn't force civilians to give way
to them, pushing them off the pavements; they gave
up their seats to old ladies in the Métro, they showed
affection to children and stroked their cheeks; they
had been told to act decently and they acted decently,
with shyness and application, out of discipline; at
times they even displayed a naïve goodwill that found
no outlet. And do not go imagining that the French
showed them a crushing air of contempt. Admittedly,

the immense majority of the French population abstained from all contact with the German army. But one should not forget that the Occupation was a *daily* affair. Someone who was asked what he had done under the Terror said, 'I lived . . .'. It is an answer we could all give today. For four years we lived, and the Germans lived too, in our midst, submerged, immersed in the unanimous life of the city. I could not help but smile at a photo from *La France Libre* that I was shown recently: a rough-necked, broad-shouldered German officer rifling through a tray of books on the banks of the Seine, under the cold, sad gaze of a little old bookseller sporting a very French goatee. The German has something of a swagger; he seems to be pushing his scrawny neighbour out of the frame. Beneath the image, a caption explains: 'The German defiles the banks of the Seine, once the province of poets and dreamers.' I entirely understand that the photograph is not faked but it is just a photograph, an arbitrary selection. The eye embraces a wider field: the photographer saw hundreds of French people rummaging through tens of trays and a single German, a small figure against this over-wide backdrop, a single

German leafing through an old book. A dreamer, a poet perhaps—at any rate an inoffensive character. It is this entirely inoffensive aspect that the soldiers strolling through the streets presented to us the whole time.

The crowd parted before their uniforms and closed behind them, leaving a pale, unassuming—half-expected—patch of faded green among the dark clothing of the civilians. The same daily necessities caused us to rub up against them, the same collective currents tossed and stirred us together: we squeezed up against them in the Métro, bumped into them in the dark nights. We would no doubt have killed them without any compunction, if ordered to do so. We no doubt retained the memory of our grudges and hatred but these feelings had assumed a rather abstract air and, at length, a kind of shameful, indefinable solidarity had established itself between the Parisians and these troopers who were, in the end, so similar to the French soldiers. A solidarity accompanied by no sympathy but formed, rather, by a biological habituation.

At the beginning, the mere sight of them hurt us and then, gradually, we learned not to see them; they assumed an institutional character. What rounded off

13

the sense of inoffensiveness for us was their ignorance of our language. A hundred times I heard Parisians speaking freely about politics in a cafe with a lonely German sitting just alongside, staring out blankly over a lemonade. They seemed more like furniture than people. When they stopped us, extremely politely, to ask the way—for most of us this was the only time we spoke to them—we felt more embarrassed than filled with hatred; all in all, *we were not natural.* We remembered the rule we had laid down for ourselves once and for all: never speak a word to them. But, at the same time, when faced with these lost soldiers, an old humanitarian helpfulness stirred in us, another rule that went back to our childhood, commanding us never to leave another human being in difficulty. Then we would decide, according to our mood or the occasion. We would say, 'I don't know' or 'Take the second left.' Either way, we went off feeling unhappy with ourselves. Once, on the Boulevard Saint-Germain, a military car overturned on top of a German colonel. I saw ten French people rush to pull him out. They hated the occupying forces, I'm sure; and among them, there would certainly be some who, two years

later, were in the F. F. I., sniping along this same boulevard. But was this man lying crushed beneath his vehicle an occupier? And what were they to do? The
concept of enemy is only entirely firm and clear when
the enemy is separated from us by a wall of fire.

Yet there was an enemy—and the most detestable
of enemies—but it had no face. Or at least those who
saw it seldom returned to describe it. I would compare
it to a tentacular monster. It seized upon our best men
in the shadows and spirited them away. It seemed that
people were silently gobbled up around us. You would
phone a friend one day and the telephone would ring
and ring in the empty apartment; you would ring his
doorbell and he wouldn't come to the door; if the
concierge broke in, you would find two chairs drawn
up together in the hallway with German cigarette ends
between the legs. When they had been present at the
arrests, the wives and mothers of the disappeared
would report that they had been taken away by very
polite Germans, similar to those who asked for directions in the street. And when they went to enquire
after them at avenue Foch or the rue des Saussaies,
they were received with courtesy and sometimes came

away with words of reassurance. In the avenue Foch, however, or the rue des Saussaies, howls of pain and terror were heard from the neighbouring buildings all day and late into the night. There was no one in Paris who had not had a relative or a friend arrested or sent to the camps or shot. There seemed to be hidden holes in the city and it seemed to empty itself through these holes, as though it had some undetectable internal haemorrhage. We did not talk about it much, in fact; we covered up this uninterrupted bloodletting even more than we did the hunger, partly out of caution and partly for reasons of dignity. We said, 'They've arrested him' and this 'they', similar to that used at times by madmen to name their fictitious persecutors, barely referred to human beings: it referred more to a kind of intangible, living tar that blackened everything, even the light.

At night we heard *them*. Around midnight, the isolated canterings of laggards resounded on the roadway as they tried to get home before the curfew, and then there was silence. And we knew that the only footsteps clattering outside were *theirs*. It is difficult to convey the impression this deserted city could give, this no-man's land pressed against our windows peopled by them alone. The houses were never entirely a defence. The Gestapo often made its arrests between midnight and 5 a.m. It seemed the door could open at any moment, letting in a cold blast of air, a little of the night and three affable Germans with revolvers. Even when we didn't name them, even when we were not thinking of them, their presence was among us. We felt it in the particular way objects had of being less our own; they were stranger, colder, more public, so to speak, as though a foreign gaze violated the privacy of our homes.

In the morning, we came upon innocent little Germans in the streets hurrying towards their offices, briefcases under their arms, looking more like uniformed lawyers than soldiers. In these familiar, expressionless faces we tried to find a little of the hateful ferocity we had imagined during the night. In vain. Yet the horror did not dissipate; and this was perhaps the most painful thing, this abstract horror that never quite settled itself on anyone. This was, in any event, the first aspect of the Occupation. Try to imagine, then, this perpetual coexistence of a phantom hatred and an over-familiar enemy whom one cannot quite come to hate.

This horror had many other causes. But, before we go further, let us avoid one misunderstanding: it should not be imagined as an overwhelming, keen emotion. I have already said: *we lived.* This means one could work, eat, chat, sleep and sometimes even laugh—even though laughter was quite rare. The horror seemed to be outside—in things. You could distract yourself from it for a moment, be excited by something you were reading, by a conversation, an affair, but you always came back to it; you realized it had not gone away. Calm and stable, almost discreet, it coloured our daydreams as it did our most practical thoughts. It was at once the weft of our consciousness and the meaning of the world. Today, when it has dissipated, we see it only as one element in our lives; but when we were immersed in it, it was so familiar that we took it sometimes for the natural tonality of our moods. Will I be understood if I say that it was intolerable and, at the same time, we got along with it very well?

Some madmen, they say, are obsessed by the feel
ing that an atrocious event has turned their lives up-
side down. And when they try to understand what
gave them such a strong impression of a break between past and present, they can find nothing. Nothing had happened. This was roughly how it was with
us. We felt at every moment that a link with the past
had been broken. Traditions were interrupted, habits
too. And we did not clearly grasp the sense of this
change, which defeat itself did not entirely explain.
Today I can see what it was: Paris was dead. There
were no cars any more, no passers-by in the streets
except at certain times in certain districts. We walked
between stones; it seemed we were left behind from
some mass exodus. A little provincial life had stuck to
the corners of the capital; there remained the skeleton
of a city, pompous and immobile, too long and too
wide for us. The streets, which you could see down
right into the far distance, were too wide; the distances
were too great; the perspectives too vast: you lost
yourself in them. The Parisians stayed at home or led
their lives in the immediate locality, for fear of moving
between these great severe palaces which were
plunged, every evening, into absolute darkness.

Here again, we must avoid exaggeration: many of us loved the village-like tranquility, the dated charm that came over this battered capital in the moonlight; but that very pleasure was tinged with bitterness: what can be more bitter than to walk in *your own* street, around *your own* church, *your own* town-hall and taste the same melancholy joy as you do when you visit the Coliseum or the Parthenon by moonlight? There was nothing but ruins: shuttered, uninhabited houses in the sixteenth arrondissement, requisitioned hotels and cinemas, indicated by white barriers which you suddenly bumped up against, shops and bars closed for the duration, their owners sent to camps, dead or disappeared, plinths with no statues, parks partly barricaded off or disfigured by reinforced concrete pillboxes, and all these big dusty letters on the tops of the buildings, neon signs that no longer light up. In the shop windows you read advertisements that seemed engraved on tombstones: all-day *sauerkraut*, Viennese patisserie, weekends at Le Touquet, everything for the car.

But *we* had all that too, you will say. In London, too, you had the blackout and the restrictions. This I know very well. But these changes in your life did not have the same meaning as the changes in ours. Though mutilated, though functioning on stand-by, London remained the capital of Britain. Paris was no longer the capital of France. All roads, all railways had led to Paris; the Parisian was at home at the centre of France, at the centre of the world. On the horizon of all his ambitions, of all his desires were New York, Madrid and London. Nourished by the Périgord, the Beauce, Alsace and the Atlantic fisheries, the capital was not, unlike ancient Rome, a parasitic city; it regulated the trade and the life of the Nation; it worked up the raw materials; it was the hub of France. With the Armistice, everything changed: the division of the country into two zones cut Paris off from the countryside; the coasts of Brittany and Normandy became forbidden zones; and a wall of concrete separated France from Britain and America. Europe remained, but Europe was a word that spelled horror; it meant servitude. The city of kings had lost even its political function, stripped of it by a phantom government at Vichy. France, divided by the Occupation into sealed provinces, had forgotten Paris.

The City was now merely a vast, flat, useless con-
glomeration, haunted by the memories of its greatness and sustained by intermittent injections. It owed
its listless life to the number of goods wagons and
lorries the Germans decided to let through each week.
If Vichy sulked a little, if Laval made them twist his
arm for Berlin's quota of French workers, the injections came to an immediate stop. Paris wilted and
yawned with hunger beneath the empty sky. Cut off
from the world, fed out of pity or by calculation, it
had now merely an abstract, symbolic existence.

A thousand times in these last four years, French
people have seen serried rows of bottles of Saint-
Emilion or Meursault in the grocers' windows. Ap-
proaching, tantalized, they found a notice saying
'dummy display'. So it was with Paris: it was merely a
dummy display. Everything was hollow and empty:
the Louvre had no paintings, the Chamber no
deputies, the Senate no senators and the lycée Mon-
taigne no pupils. It was the purpose of the artificial
existence the Germans maintained there—the theatri-
cal performances, the horse-races, the miserable,
lugubrious festivals—to show the world that France

was intact because Paris was still alive. A strange consequence of centralization. The British, for their part, while flattening Lorient, Rouen or Nantes with their bombs, had decided to respect Paris. Thus, in this dying city, we enjoyed a symbolic, funereal calm. Around this islet of peace, iron and fire rained down; but, just as we were not permitted to share the labour of our provinces, we were no longer entitled to share their suffering. A symbol: this hard-working, quick-tempered city was now nothing but a symbol. We looked at each other and wondered whether we had not become symbols ourselves.

The fact is that, for four years our future had been stolen from us. We had to rely on the others. And for the others we were merely an *object*. Doubtless, the British press and radio showed us friendship. But we would have had to have been very presumptuous or very naïve to believe that the British were pursuing this murderous war with the aim of freeing us. They were defending their vital interests, and doing so manfully, bearing arms, and we well knew that we entered into their calculations only as one factor among others. As for the Germans, they were contemplating the best way to incorporate this piece of land into the 'European' bloc. We could feel our destiny slipping away from us; France was like a pot of flowers that you put on the window ledge when it is sunny and bring in again at night without a 'by your leave'.

Everyone knows those sick individuals who are termed 'depersonalized', and who suddenly come to believe that all human beings are dead because they have stopped projecting their own futures forward and have, as a result, lost any sense of other peoples'. Perhaps the most painful thing was that all Parisians were depersonalized. Before the war, if we happened to look sympathetically on a child or young person, we did so because we sensed their future, because we obscurely divined it from their gestures and the lines on their faces. For a living human being is, above all, a project, an undertaking. But the Occupation stripped human beings of their futures. Never again did we gaze after a young couple, attempting to imagine their destiny: we had no more destiny than a nail or a doorknob. All our acts were provisional, their meaning confined to the day they were performed. Workers worked in the factories with no thought for the morrow: the next day there may be no electricity, the Germans may stop sending raw materials, they may decide suddenly to deport them to Bavaria or the Palatinate; students prepared for their exams, but who would have dared say with certainty that they could sit them?

We looked at each other and it seemed we were seeing the dead. This dehumanization and petrification was so intolerable that many, to escape it and regain a future, threw themselves into the Resistance. A strange future, barred by torture, prison and death, but a future we were at last producing with our own hands.[1] Yet Resistance was merely an individual solution and we always knew this: without it the British would still have won the war, with it they would still have lost it, if that was how it was meant to be. First and foremost, it had a symbolic value for us; and that is why many resisters were in despair: still just symbols. A symbolic rebellion in a symbolic city; only the tortures were real.

So we felt out of it. We were ashamed at not understanding this war that we were no longer fighting. We watched from afar as the British and Russians adapted to the German tactics, while continuing to ruminate on our defeat of 1940. It had been too quick and we had learned nothing from it. Those who congratulate us ironically on having escaped the war cannot imagine how ardently the French would have liked to take up arms again. Day after day we saw our towns and cities destroyed, our wealth obliterated; our young people wasted away; three million of us were rotting in Germany; the French birth rate was falling. What battle could have been more destructive? But these sacrifices, which we would have made willingly if they would have hastened our victory, had no meaning and were of no use except to the Germans. And this, perhaps, everyone will understand: what is terrible is not to suffer or die, but to suffer or die in vain.

In our absolute abandonment, we saw from time to time Allied planes flying overhead. Our situation was so paradoxical that the siren warned us of them as enemies. We were under strict orders: you had to leave your office, close your shop and go down to the shelters. We never obeyed: we stayed in the streets looking up into the sky. And this indiscipline should not be seen as empty revolt or a silly affectation of courage: we were desperately watching the only friends we still had.

This young pilot in his plane above over our heads was connected to Britain, to America, by invisible bonds; it was an enormous free world that filled the sky. But the only messages he bore were messages of death.

You will never know what faith in our allies it took to continue to love them, *to want with them* the destruction they wrought on our soil, to hail their bombers, in spite of everything, as the face of Britain. If bombs missed their targets and fell on an urban area, we went to enormous lengths to find excuses; sometimes we even accused the Germans of dropping them, to turn us against Britain, or of deliberately sounding the alarm too late. I spent a few days at Le Havre with the family of one of my fellow POWs, during the spell of heavy bombing. The first evening we were gathered round the wireless, the father twiddling the buttons with a naïve, touching solemnity; you would have thought he was celebrating mass. And, as the BBC gave us its first news, we heard a faraway roar of aircraft. We knew very well they were coming to drop their bombs on us. I shall not soon forget the mixture of terror and delight in the hushed tones of one of the women, as she said, 'Here come the British!' And for a quarter of an hour, without moving from their seats, to the sound of explosions all around, they listened to the voice of London; it seemed to them to be more present, and that the squadrons moving above our heads lent body to it.

But these acts of faith put us under perpetual tension: they often required us to suppress our indignation. We suppressed it when Lorient was razed to the ground, when the centre of Nantes was destroyed, when the heart of Rouen was hit. Perhaps you will divine the effort this took. Sometimes anger got the upper hand—and then we tried to reason things out, as you would over a passion. I remember, in July 1944, the train bringing me from Chantilly was machine-gunned. It was a harmless little suburban train; three planes passed overhead and in a matter of seconds there were three dead and twelve wounded in the front carriage. The passengers, standing on the track, watched as the stretchers went by, along with some green benches that had been brought from the platforms of the neighbouring station because there were not enough stretchers to carry all the bodies. They were white with anger and emotion. You were insulted, you were called inhuman and barbaric: 'Why do they have to attack a defenceless train? Isn't there enough for them to do across the Rhine? Let them go to Berlin! Don't like the anti-aircraft guns, do they?' and so on. Then, suddenly, someone found an explanation. 'Listen, normally they attack the engine and no one gets wounded. Only today the loco was at the back, so they shot at the front carriage. At the speed they were going, they didn't spot the change.' Immediately everyone fell silent. The people were relieved that the pilot had not committed an unforgiveable crime, because we could continue to love you. But this temptation to hate you was not the least of our misfortunes, and we often had to fight against it. And I can testify that on the days when we watched the smoke from the fires you had lit on the outskirts of the city, with the Germans, our conquerors, looking on sardonically, we felt totally alone.

Yet we did not dare complain: we had bad consciences. I first knew the secret shame that tormented us when I was a POW. The prisoners were unhappy, but they could not go so far as to pity themselves.

'Well,' they said, 'we're really going to cop it when we get home!' Their pain was keen and bitter; theirs was a disagreeable suffering, poisoned by the sense of having deserved it. They were ashamed before France. But France was ashamed before the world. It is pleasant to weep a little over your own fate. But how could we have found pity for ourselves when we were surrounded by other people's scorn. The Poles in my *Stalag* did not conceal their contempt; the Czechs condemned us for having abandoned them in [19]38; I heard a report of an escaped Russian, hidden by a gendarme in Anjou, who said of us, with a fond smile, 'The French? Rabbits! rabbits!'

You have not always been that gentle on us yourselves and I remember a particular speech by Marshal Smuts that we had to listen to in silence. After that, of course, we were tempted to cling to our humiliation, to wallow in it. Perhaps it would have been possible to defend ourselves. After all, the world's three greatest powers took four years to overcome Germany; was it not natural that we would give in at the first onslaught, having no one's help to withstand it? But it did not enter our minds to plead: the best of us joined the Resistance out of a need to redeem our country. The others remained hesitant and ill-at-ease; they ruminated on their inferiority complex. Do you not think this the worst of hardships—the one you suffer without being able to judge it undeserved or regard it as redemptive?

But just as we were going to give in to remorse, the Vichyites and collaborators, by attempting to push us in that direction, held us back. The Occupation was not just this constant presence of the conquerors in our towns and cities, it was also, on all the walls and in the newspapers, this vile image of ourselves they were trying to foist on us. The collaborators began by appealing to our good-heartedness. 'We are defeated,' they said, 'let's show that we're good losers: let's acknowledge our failings.' And, immediately afterwards, 'Let's agree that the Frenchman is flippant, scatter-brained, boastful and selfish, that he understands nothing of foreign nations and that the war caught our country falling to pieces.' Comic posters ridiculed our last hopes. Faced with so much baseness and such crude tricks, we stiffened; we wanted to be proud of ourselves. Alas, no sooner had we raised our heads than we rediscovered in ourselves our true grounds for remorse. And so we lived in the worst disarray, unhappy without daring to admit it to ourselves, ashamed and yet disgusted with our shame.

And, to cap it all, we could not take a step, eat or even breathe without colluding with the occupier. Before the war, the pacifists had explained on more than one occasion that an invaded country must refuse to fight and must exert passive resistance. This is easy to say. But, for that resistance to be effective, the railwayman would have had to refuse to drive his train, the farmer would have had to refuse to plough his field. The conqueror would perhaps have been inconvenienced, though he could bring supplies from his own country, but the Occupied nation would have been certain of perishing in its entirety in short order. We had to work, then; we had to keep up a semblance of economic organization for the nation, had to maintain, despite the destruction and the looting, a minimum living standard. Yet the slightest activity served the enemy, who had descended on us and stuck his leeches on our skin and lived in symbiosis with us. Not a drop of blood formed in our veins in which he did not share.

There has been much said of 'collaborators' and there were, admittedly, some genuine traitors among us: we are not ashamed of them; every nation has its dregs, that fringe of failures and the embittered who momentarily take advantage of disasters and revolutions. The existence of Quisling and Laval in a population is a *normal* phenomenon, like the suicide or the crime rate. But what seemed abnormal to us was the situation of the country, which was wholly collaborationist. The *maquisards*, who were our pride and joy, were not working for the enemy, but if the peasants wanted to feed them, they had to go on raising livestock, half of which went to Germany. Every one of our acts was ambiguous: we never knew whether to condemn ourselves totally or fully approve our actions; a subtle poison infected the best of undertakings.

I shall give just one example: the railwaymen, both the stokers and the drivers, were admirable. Their sangfroid, courage and, often, their self-sacrifice saved lives by the hundreds and enabled trains to reach Paris. For the most part, they were resisters and have proved it. Yet the zeal with which they defended our equipment served the German cause: these miraculously preserved locomotives could be requisitioned at the drop of a hat. Among the human lives they saved, you had to count those of the troops on their way to Le Havre or Cherbourg; and the trains bringing food supplies were also carrying war *matériel*. And so these men, who were concerned only to serve their compatriots, were, by force of circumstance, on the side of our enemies against our friends. And when Pétain stuck a medal on their chests, it was Germany that was decorating them. From one end of the war to the other, we did not *recognize* our acts; we were not able to claim their consequences as our own. Evil was everywhere; any choice was bad and yet we had to choose and we were responsible; every beat of our hearts drove us further into a horrifying state of guilt.

Perhaps we would have borne better the abject condition to which we were reduced if we had been able to achieve that unity against Vichy that Vichy constantly called for. But it is not true that misfortune unites. First of all, the Occupation scattered families to the four winds. A particular Paris industrialist, for example, had left his wife and daughter in the *zone libre* and—at least for the first two years—could not see them again or write them anything but postcards; his elder son was a prisoner in an *Oflag*, his younger son had joined de Gaulle. Paris was a city of absentees and the cult of memory we practised for four years was perhaps one of the more striking aspects of our situation; it was a cult directed, through our distant friends, to a sweetness of life and a pride in living that had now disappeared.

Despite our efforts, the memories paled more each day, the faces faded one by one. We talked a lot about the prisoners, then less, then even less than that. It was not that we stopped thinking about them but from having been precise, painful forms within us, they had become just gaping, empty spaces. Gradually they merged with the thinness of our blood; we missed them as we did fat, sugar or vitamins; in the same total, undifferentiated way. The taste of chocolate or *foie gras* vanished similarly, as did the memory of certain radiant days—of a 14 July at the Bastille, a walk with a loved one, an evening by the sea, or the greatness of France. And our exigencies diminished with our memories and, since one comes to terms with anything, we had the shame of coming to terms with our misery, with the swedes that were served at our tables, the tiny freedoms we still possessed, our inner emptiness. We simplified ourselves a little more each day and we ended up speaking only of food, less perhaps out of hunger or fear of the morrow and more because the pursuit of eating 'opportunities' was the only enterprise still within our scope.

And then the Occupation awakened old quarrels. It aggravated dissensions that divided French people. The splitting of France into northern and southern zones whipped up the old rivalry between Paris and the provinces again, between the North and the 'Midi'. The inhabitants of Clermont-Ferrand and Nice accused the Parisians of collusion with the enemy. The Parisians, for their part, criticized those in the *zone libre* for being 'soft' and for brazenly flaunting their selfish satisfaction at not being 'occupied'. From this point of view, it must be admitted, the Germans, by violating the clauses of the Armistice and extending the Occupation to the whole country, did us a great service: they restored the unity of the nation.

But many other conflicts persisted, such as that between town- and country-dwellers, for example. The peasants, wounded for many years by the contempt in which they believed they were held, took their revenge and held out on the city-dwellers: the latter, in return, accused them of supplying the black market and starving the urban population. The government stoked the quarrel with speeches in which the peasants were at times lauded to the skies and at others condemned for concealing their harvests. The brazenness of the luxury restaurants set the workers against the middle classes. In fact, these establishments were frequented mainly by Germans and a handful of 'collaborators', but their existence rendered social inequalities tangible.

Similarly, the working classes were only too aware that it was among them that forced labourers were recruited: the bourgeoisie was not, or was only barely, affected. Was this a German ploy to spread discord or was it not rather that manual workers were of greater use to Germany? I do not know. But, and this is a mark of our uncertainty, we did not know whether to rejoice that students largely escaped being deported or to wish, out of a sense of solidarity, that deportation would extend to all social strata. For the sake of completeness, we must mention, lastly, that the defeat

37

exacerbated the conflict between the generations. For four years, the soldiers of the '[19]14–18 war' blamed those of [19]40 for having lost the war and the soldiers of 1940, in return, blamed their elders for having lost the peace.

However, do not go imagining a France torn asunder. The truth is not so simple. These quarrels appeared mainly as obstacles to an immense, clumsy desire for union. Never perhaps was there so much goodwill. Young people dreamed obscurely of a new order; the employers were, overall, inclined to make concessions. Whenever two jostling Métro passengers came to blows, whenever a blundering pedestrian and a careless cyclist clashed, the same muttering went up from the crowd: 'How bad is that! French people quarrelling! And in front of Germans!' But, in most cases, the very circumstances of the Occupation, the barriers the Germans erected between us and the needs of clandestine struggle prevented these good intentions from finding an outlet. So these four years were a long, impotent dream of unity.

This is what lends the present moment its distressing urgency: the barriers have fallen, our fate is in our own hands. Which will win out — the old quarrels that have been reawakened or this great desire for solidarity? But from all of you watching from London, we must crave a little patience: the memory of the Occupation has not faded; we have barely awakened from it. In my case, when I come around a corner and see an American soldier, I react with a sudden, instinctive start: I take him for a German. Conversely, a German soldier, who had hidden in a cellar and wanted to surrender because he was starving, was able to ride unmolested down the Champs-Elysées on his bicycle a fortnight after the Liberation. The crowd had become so habituated that it did not *see* him. We need a lot of time to forget and tomorrow's France still has not shown its true face.

But we are asking you first to understand that the Occupation was often more terrible than the war. For in war everyone can perform his task as a human being whereas, in that ambiguous situation, we really could neither *act* nor even *think*. Unarguably, during this period—apart from the Resistance—France did not always furnish proof of its greatness. But you must first understand that active resistance was, of necessity, limited to a minority. And then it seems to me that this minority, which offered itself up for martyrdom determinedly and without hope, is amply sufficient to redeem our weaknesses. And, lastly, if these pages have helped you gauge what our country has suffered, in shame, horror and anger, I believe you will think, as I do, that even where it erred it is deserving of respect.

La France libre, published in London, 1945.

what is a collaborator?

Crown Prince Olaf, who has just returned to Norway, estimates that 'collaborators' represent two per cent of the total population. Doubtless, the percentage was fairly similar in France. A survey of the various occupied countries would enable us to establish a kind of average percentage of collaborators in contemporary communities, since collaboration, like suicide or crime, is a normal phenomenon. But in peacetime, or during wars that do not end in disaster, these elements within the community remain in a state of latency. Since the determining factors are absent, 'the collaborator' does not reveal himself, either to others or to himself, but goes about his business; he may perhaps be patriotic for he is ignorant of the nature within him which, in favourable circumstances, will one day disclose itself.

During the present war, which made it possible to *isolate* collaboration in the way that illnesses are isolated, there was a parlour game popular among the British: the aim was to sift through all of London's prominent personalities and pick out which ones would have collaborated if Britain had been invaded. It was not such a silly game, since it came down to the idea that collaboration is a vocation. In fact, in our own country, there were no great surprises. You had only to know Déat[2] or Bonnard[3] before the war to find it natural that they should join forces with the victorious Germans. If it is true, then, that people do not collaborate by chance, but under the influence of certain social and psychological laws, it seems appropriate that we should define what is known as a collaborator.

It would be a mistake to confuse the collaborator with the fascist, even though every collaborator had, on principle, to accept the ideology of the Nazis. Indeed, some notorious fascists abstained from colluding with the enemy because they felt conditions were not right for the emergence of fascism in a weakened, occupied France; former Cagoulards[4] went over to the Resistance. Conversely, a certain number of radicals, socialists and pacifists took the view that the Occupation was a lesser evil and they could get along with the Germans.

Similarly, we must be careful not to equate the collaborator with the conservative bourgeois. The bourgeoisie had, admittedly, been very half-hearted since Munich. They feared a war which, as Thierry Maulnier[5] clearly put it, would mark the triumph of the proletariat. This explains the negative attitude of certain reserve officers. But if the bourgeoisie made only a feeble effort in the war, it does not follow that they intended to surrender to Germany. All the workers and almost all the peasants were in the Resistance: most collaborators were, as a matter of fact, recruited from among the middle classes. But one should not jump to the conclusion that the bourgeoisie *as a class* favoured collaboration. To begin with, it provided many members of the Resistance: almost all the intellectuals, and a section of the industrialists and tradespeople, actively fought the occupying power.

If one were trying to define a strictly bourgeois standpoint, it would be more accurate to say that the conservative bourgeoisie was pro-Pétain and *attentiste*. It has been said that capitalism's interests are international and the French bourgeoisie would have profited by a German victory. But this is an abstract principle: in the event, what was at issue was the subordination, pure and simple, of the French economy to the German. The leading industrialists were not unaware that Germany's aim was to destroy France as an industrial power and, consequently, to destroy French capitalism. And how could the French bourgeoisie, which has always seen national autonomy as synonymous with its own sovereignty as a ruling class, not have realized that collaboration, by making France a German satellite, was contributing to wrecking bourgeois sovereignty? While they were, most often, of bourgeois origin, the collaborators turned immediately against their class. For Déat or Luchaire,[6] the Gaullist was the prototype of the bourgeois who 'doesn't get it' because he cares about his wealth.

In reality, collaboration is a phenomenon of disintegration; it was, in each case, an individual decision, not a class position. Initially, it represents a fixation by foreign collective forms of elements poorly assimilated by the indigenous community. It is in this respect that it is akin to criminality and suicide, which are also phenomena of disassimilation. Wherever social life remained intense, in hotbeds of religion or politics, there was no place for these phenomena; as soon as various factors intervened and created a sort of social hesitancy, they appeared.

We may, then, attempt a broad classification of the collaborators. They were recruited from the marginal elements of the major political parties, examples being Déat and Marquet,[7] who were not able to settle in the Socialist Party (La Section Française de l'Internationale Ouvrière), and Doriot,[8] who was expelled from the Communist Party. And from among the intellectuals who loathed the bourgeoisie, their class of origin, but did not have the courage, or simply the opportunity, to join the proletariat—examples here being Drieu la Rochelle,[9] who had a lifelong obsession with both Italian Fascism and Russian Communism, and Ramon Fernandez[10] who was close to communism for a while but abandoned the Communist Party for the

PPF because, as he put it, 'I prefer trains that are de-
parting' (this perpetual oscillation between fascism and
communism is typical of the disintegrative forces at
work in the marginal zones of the bourgeoisie). Failures
in journalism, the arts or the teaching profession make
up another category, as in the case of Alain
Laubreaux,[11] who was a critic on *Je Suis Partout*.[12] Having
arrived from Nouméa (New Caledonia) hoping to take
Paris by storm, he never gained acceptance and, after
being floored on his arrival in France by a trial for pla-
giarism, he wavered for a long time between Right and
Left, was a disloyal secretary to Henri Béraud[13] and
subsequently a staff writer on *La Dépêche de Toulouse*, the
great Radical–Socialist newspaper of the South-West,
before ending up in the ranks of the French neo-
fascists.

But in a community there are not just individual
cases of disintegration: whole groups may be
wrenched from the collectivity by forces exerted on
them from outside. For example, it is ultramontanism
that explains the collaborationist attitude of certain
members of the higher clergy. Even before they came
into contact with the occupying powers, they felt a

kind of attraction towards Rome that acted as an un-
balancing force. By contrast, the lower clergy, solidly
rooted in French soil and of a Gallican persuasion far
removed from Rome, turned out as a whole to be
fierce resisters. Most importantly, for want of the will
or capacity fully to implement its principles, the
French Revolution left in existence on the fringes of
the democratic community an outcast element that
has survived into our own day. It would be an exaggeration to argue, as some have, that France has been
cut in two since 1789. But, in fact, while the majority
of bourgeois came to terms with a capitalist democracy that enshrined the free-enterprise regime, a small
section of the bourgeois class remained outside
French national life because it refused to adapt to the
republican constitution. For the 'internal exiles', the
royalists of Action française[14] or the fascists of *Je Suis
Partout*, France's collapse in 1940 meant first and foremost the end of the Republic. Having no real ties with
contemporary France, with our great political traditions, with a century and a half of our history and culture, there was nothing to protect them from the force
of attraction exerted by a foreign community.

47

It is in this way that we can explain this curious paradox: the majority of collaborators were recruited from among what have been dubbed 'Right-wing anarchists'. They accepted none of the Republic's laws, declared themselves free to reject taxation or war, resorted to violence against their opponents despite the rights recognized by our constitution. And yet they based their indiscipline and violence on a conception of a rigorous order; and when they offered their services to a foreign power, it was quite naturally the case that that power was subject to a dictatorial regime. The fact is that these elements, whose anarchy was merely a mark of their profound disintegration, had always wished, in compensation, for a radical integration, precisely because their disintegration was something *suffered*, not desired. They have never taken responsibility for their anarchic freedom, never taken ownership of it; they did not have the courage to draw the logical consequences from their rigorously individualist attitudes. Rather, they kept up, on the margins of actual society, the dream of an authoritarian society into which they could merge and integrate themselves. So they preferred the order the German state seemed to represent for them to the national re ality from which they were excluded.

So no class, as such, bears the responsibility for collaboration. And collaboration is not even indicative, as has been argued, of a weakening of the democratic ideal: it merely shows up the effects, within contemporary communities, of the normal play of the social forces of disintegration. The socially outcast element, which is practically negligible in peacetime, becomes very important in cases of defeat followed by occupation. It would be unjust to call the bourgeoisie a collaborator 'class'. But we can, and must, judge it as a class by the fact that the collaborators were recruited almost exclusively from within it. This is sufficient to show that it has lost its ideology, its force and its internal cohesion.

It is not enough just to have determined the social space of collaboration: there is a psychology of the collaborator from which we can draw some precious lessons. We may, of course, decide from the outset that treason is always motivated by self-interest and ambition. But, though that broad-brush psychology perhaps makes classification and condemnation easier, it does not entirely correspond to reality. There were disinterested collaborators who silently wished for a German victory without deriving any advantage from their sympathies. Most of those who wrote for the press or took positions in government were, admittedly, ambitious and unscrupulous, but there were also some who occupied positions before the war that were important enough to spare them the need for treason.

And what a strange ambition: if this passion is, ultimately, the pursuit of absolute power over human beings, there was a glaring contradiction in the ambition of the collaborator who, even if he had been made leader of the French pseudo-government, could only ever have been an agent of transmission. It was not his personal prestige but the force of the occupying armies that gave him his authority. Maintained in place by foreign armies, he could only be the agent of an alien power. Though apparently first among the French, he would, if Nazism had triumphed, have been only the thousandth most important man in Europe. Real ambition, if moral principles had not sufficed, ought to have led him to join the Resistance:

the leader of a little band of *maquisards* had more scope for action, more prestige and real authority than Laval ever had. If we want to understand the attitude of the collaborators we must, then, examine them dispassionately and describe them objectively on the basis of their words and deeds.

Self-evidently, they all believed, primarily, in a German victory. One cannot imagine a journalist, writer, industrialist or politician who would have chosen to profit from the advantages of Occupation only for four years, knowing or sensing that his escapade would end in imprisonment or death. But this intellectual error, which enables us to understand their attitude, cannot be a justification for it. I knew lots of people in 1940 who thought Britain was finished; the weak gave in to despair, others walled themselves up in an ivory tower and yet others, out of truth to their principles, commenced resistance, taking the view that Germany had won the war but that it was within their power to make it lose the peace. If the collaborators concluded from the Germany victory that it was necessary to subject themselves to the authority of the Reich, this was because they had already taken a profound, original decision that formed the bedrock of their personality: the decision to bow to the fait accompli, whatever it may be. This initial tendency, which they themselves adorned with the name of 'realism', has deep roots in the ideology of our times.

The collaborator suffers from that intellectual illness that may be called historicism. And history does indeed teach us that a great collective event, as soon as it appears, arouses hatred and resistance, which, though sometimes very fine, will later be regarded as ineffectual. As the collaborators saw it, those who devoted their lives to a lost cause may well be seen as fine figures of men, but they were, nonetheless, behind the times and out of step with reality. Such people die twice, because the principles by which they lived are also buried with them. By contrast, the promoters of the historical event, be they Caesar, Napoleon or Henry Ford, will perhaps meet with opprobrium in their own day from the standpoint of a particular ethics, but fifty or a hundred years later only their effectiveness will be remembered and they will be judged by principles they themselves laid down.

A hundred times, among the most honest professors of history and in the most objective of books, I have found this tendency to ratify events simply because they have occurred. They are here confusing the need, insofar as they are scholars, to submit to the facts, with a certain inclination, insofar as they are moral agents, to approve those facts morally. The collaborators took over this philosophy of history. For them, the dominion of the facts went together with a vague belief in progress, but a decapitated progress. The classical notion of progress in fact assumes an ascent that carries it continually towards an ideal endpoint. The collaborators regard themselves as too matter-of-fact to believe, without evidence, in this ideal end-point and, hence to believe in the meaning of history. But, though they reject these metaphysical interpretations in the name of science, they do not, for all that, abandon the idea of progress: it merges, in their view, with the march of history. They do not know where they are going but, since they are changing, they must be getting better. The latest historical phenomenon is the best simply because it is the latest: they dimly perceive that it contributes to shaping the face of humanity, that rough sketch which, with each passing moment, acquires a new inflection; they are seized by a kind of pithiatism, abandon themselves passively to the various emerging currents and float towards an unknown destination; they experience the delights of not thinking, of not looking ahead and of accepting the obscure transformations that necessarily turn us into new and unpredictable human beings.

Realism here conceals the fear of performing the customary work of the human being—that stubborn, narrow work that consists in saying 'yes' or 'no' in accordance with principles, in 'undertaking without hope and persevering without success'—and a mystical appetite for mystery, a docile attitude towards a future one has stopped trying to shape; one confines oneself merely to foretelling. Poorly digested Hegelianism has, of course, its part to play in this too. Violence is accepted because all great changes are based on violence and an obscure moral virtue is ascribed to force. Thus, in the assessment of his actions, the collaborator positions himself in the most distant future. His moving closer to Germany, in opposition to Britain, seemed to us a failure to honour a commitment, an unjustifiable breach of his word. The collaborator, though living in our century, judged it from the standpoint of future centuries, precisely as the historian judges the policies of Frederick II. He had found a name for it; it was, quite simply, a 'reversal of alliances' for which there were numerous precedents in history.

This way of judging events in the light of the future was, I think, one of the temptations of defeat for all French people. It represented a subtle form of escapism. By jumping forward a few centuries and, from thence, looking back on the present to contemplate it from afar and resituate it in history, one helped turn it into something past and disguise its unbearable character. The desire was to forget a crushing defeat by envisaging it only in terms of its historical consequences. But this was to forget that history, though it is understood retrospectively and in great swathes, is something that is lived and made day by day. This choice of the historicist attitude and this continual 'pastifying' of the present are typical of the collaborators.

The least guilty are disillusioned idealists who, weary of proposing their ideals in vain, came suddenly to believe that they had to be imposed. If, for example, so many collaborators came from French pacifist ranks, that is because the pacifists, incapable of staving off war, had suddenly decided to see the German army as the force that would bring about peace. Their method had, until that point, been one of propaganda and education. It had proved ineffective. So they persuaded themselves that they were merely changing their methods: they transported themselves into the future to judge present events and, from thence, they saw the Nazi victory bringing a *pax germanica* to the world that was comparable with the famous *pax romana*. The conflict with Russia, then with America, did not open their eyes: they saw these simply as necessary evils. Thus was born one of the most curious paradoxes of our times: the alliance between the most ardent pacifists and the soldiers of a warrior society.

By his docile attitude to facts—or, rather to the single fact of French defeat—the 'realist' collaborator produces an inverted morality: instead of judging facts in the light of what is right, he bases what is right upon what *is*. His implicit metaphysics identifies *is* with *ought*. All that *is* is good; what is good is what *is*.

On these principles he hastily builds an ethics of man-
liness. Borrowing from Descartes the maxim, 'Attempt to conquer yourself, rather than the world', he
thinks submission to the facts schools him in courage
and manly toughness. In his view, whatever does not
start out from an objective appreciation of the situation is the mere fantasy of women and daydreamers.
He explains the Resistance not in terms of the assertion of values, but as an anachronistic attachment to
dead ways and a dead ideology.

Yet he conceals from himself this deep-seated
contradiction: that he too has *chosen* the facts on which
he bases his position. The military power of Russia,
the industrial power of America, the stubborn resistance of Britain under the 'blitz', the revolt of the
enslaved Europeans and the aspiration of human
beings to dignity and freedom are also facts. But he
has chosen, in the name of realism, not to take account of them. Hence the internal weakness of his
system: this man who talks constantly of the 'hard
lessons of fact' has selected only those facts
favourable to his doctrine. He is perpetually dishonest
in his haste to set inconvenient facts aside. A fortnight

after the German armies entered Russia, for example, Marcel Déat happily wrote: 'Now that the Russian colossus has collapsed . . .'.

Believing German victory to be achieved already, the collaborator aims to replace legal relations of reciprocity and equality between nations by a kind of feudal bond between suzerain and vassal. Alphonse de Châteaubriant[15] sees himself as Hitler's liege man. Not being integrated into French society and subject to the universal laws of a community, collaborators attempt to integrate themselves into a new system in which relationships obtain solely on a singular, person-to-person basis. Their realism helps them to do this: the cult of the singular fact and the contempt for Right, which is a universal, leads them to submit themselves to rigorously individual realities: a man, a party or a foreign nation.

As a result, the collaborator's morality, which is variable and contradictory, will be pure obedience to the suzerain's whim. Déat contradicts himself a hundred times, depending on the orders that come down to him from Abetz.[16] He is untroubled by this: the coherence of his attitude consists precisely in changing his point of view as often as his master wishes. But this feudal submission is not itself without its deep contradictions.

If Machiavelli is the dictators' guru, Talleyrand is the model for collaborators. The ambitious collaborator contents himself with a subordinate role, but this is because he believes he has a hand he can play. His loyalty to Germany is conditional. During the Occupation, how many Vichy or Paris politicians kept saying: 'The Germans are children. They have an inferiority complex where France is concerned: we'll do with them as we like'? Some envisaged taking over the 'star supporting role' from the Italians; others took the view that their hour would come when Germany and America would want a third power to open negotiations between them.

Having settled on *force* as the source of Right and as the master's prerogative, the collaborators saw *cunning* as theirs. They recognized their weakness, then, and these high priests of manly power and masculine virtues adapted to using the weapons of the weak—women's weapons. Throughout the articles of Châteaubriant, Drieu and Brasillach,[17] one finds curious metaphors that present relations between France and Germany from the angle of a sexual union in which France plays the female role. And the feudal bond between the collaborator and his master very definitely has a sexual aspect to it.

Insofar as one can imagine the collaborators' state of mind, one senses something like a climate of femininity. The collaborator speaks in terms of force, but he does not possess force. He has the cunning and shrewdness that leans on force; he even has charm and seductiveness, since he claims to play on the attraction French culture exerts, in his view, on the Germans. It seems to me there is a strange mixture of masochism and homosexuality here. And Parisian homosexual circles provided many a brilliant recruit.

However, what perhaps amounts to the best psychological explanation of collaboration is hatred. The collaborator seems to dream of a strict feudal order: as we have said, this is the great dream of assimilation for an element of the community that has split away. But it is merely a pipe dream. He actually hates this society, in which he has not been able to play a role. If he dreams of submitting it to the fascist yoke, he does so to enslave it and reduce it practically to the state of a machine. It is typical that Déat, Luchaire and Darnand[18] were perfectly aware of their unpopularity. A hundred times they wrote with absolute lucidity that the immense majority of the country disapproved of their policies. But they had no thought of deploring the indignation and fury they aroused: they needed them. Through that indignation and fury, they brought into being, as an impotent and vainly rebellious totality beneath them, that French community into which they had been unable to merge—which excluded them. Since they could not succeed within that community from the inside, they would bring it to heel from the outside; to violate that proud nation, they would integrate themselves into German Europe. Being Hitler's slaves mattered little to them if they could infect the whole of France with that slavery. This was the particular nature of their ambition.

With Drieu la Rochelle, things were not so simple: he started out by hating himself. For twenty years he depicted himself as unhinged, a split personality, a waste of space, dreaming of an iron discipline for himself that he could not spontaneously provide. But, as his novel *Gilles* attests, this self-hatred became a hatred of humanity. Unable to bear the harsh truth that he was 'a weak, spineless child', incapable of mastering his passions, he tried to see himself as a typical product of an entirely rotten society. He dreamt of fascism for that society, whereas all that was needed was to lay down some strict rules of conduct for himself. He wanted to eliminate the human element from himself and others by transforming human societies into anthills. For this pessimist, the coming of fascism corresponded, ultimately, to the suicide of humanity.

Realism, rejection of the universal, anarchy and the dream of an iron discipline, the defence of violence and cunning, femininity, hatred of humanity— so many characteristics that can be explained by disintegration. The collaborator, whether or not he has the opportunity to manifest himself as such, is an enemy democratic societies perpetually carry within them. If we want to avoid that enemy surviving the war in other forms, it is not enough just to execute a few traitors. We must, as far as possible, complete the unification of French society or, in other words, the task begun by the 1789 Revolution. And this can be achieved only by a new revolution, the one that was attempted in 1830, 1848 and 1871 and which was always followed by counter-revolution. Democracy has always been a nursery for fascists because, by its nature, it tolerates all opinions. We should, at last, pass some restrictive laws: there must be no freedom to oppose freedom.

And since the collaborator's favourite argument—and the fascist's—is *realism*, we should take advantage of our victory to confirm the failure of all realist politics. One ought, of course, to come to terms with the facts, to draw lessons from experience. But this flexibility, this political positivism must be only a means for achieving an end that is not subordinate to the facts and that does not derive its existence from them. By providing the example of a politics based on principles, we shall be contributing to ridding the world of the species of 'pseudo-realists'. By contrast, the Resistance, which won out in the end, has shown that the role of human beings is to know how to say 'no' to the facts, even when it seems one must bow down before them.

Admittedly, one has to try to conquer oneself rather than vanquish fortune but if one has to conquer oneself first, one does so, ultimately, the better to vanquish fortune.

La République française, published in New York, August 1945.

the end of the war

People had been told to put out flags. They did not. The war ended in indifference and anxiety.

Nothing had changed in everyday life. The booming of the radio, the bold type of the newspapers were not able to persuade us. We would have liked some sort of marvel, a sign in the heavens, to prove to us that peace had written itself into things. A puny gun coughed on a boring summer's afternoon. People went by on the bridges and in the streets with lifeless eyes, busy with their chronic hunger and their own concerns.

How are we, with our empty stomachs, to rejoice at the end of this war that just goes on ending and which, after ravaging our land, has gone off to die at the back of beyond, around those islands whose name reminds us of double almonds and family betting games.[19] And what an abstract end. There may, it seems, be turmoil in Japan; the Japanese army is counter-attacking in Manchuria and the emperor and his captains speak of impending revenge; the Chinese are on the verge of civil war. And, in the background, immense emergent powers eye each other with some surprise and a formal coldness, weighing each other up and keeping a respectful distance, like those wrestlers who rapidly stroke each other's forearms and shoulders before coming to grips.

Yet certain men in their offices have decided the war is over. One of them announces it, speaking at a microphone, a piece of paper in his hand. To believe him, we would have had not to have learned to disbelieve the words of men who come to microphones with pieces of paper in their hands. It is not that one dares imagine he is lying. One merely thinks this whole business of war and peace unfolds at a certain level of truth: the truth of historical declarations, military parades and commemorative ceremonies. People

look at each other with a vague sense of disappoint-
ment: is this all that Peace is?

It isn't Peace. Peace is a beginning. We are living
through death throes. For a long time we thought War
and Peace were two clearly distinct entities, like Black
and White or Hot and Cold. It wasn't true and today we
know it. Between 1934 and 1939, we learned that Peace
can end without war breaking out. We are familiar with
the exquisite subtleties of armed neutrality, intervention
and pre-belligerency. The movement from peace to war
in our century is a matter of continuous gradations. On
the most optimistic view, we are going to have to go
through this process in the opposite direction. Today,
20 August 1945, in this deserted, starving Paris, the War
has ended but Peace has not begun.

Peace seemed to us like a *return*. A return of the
roaring twenties, a return of French prosperity and
greatness. In wartime, people always look forward to
the peace of their youth: they confuse youth and
peace. It is always a different peace that comes. The
one that is vaguely in the air now, beyond the final
storms, is an enormous world peace, in which France
has only a very small place.

The little gun that was coughing the other afternoon confirmed France's slide—and that of Europe. A verdict delivered at the other end of the earth told us that the time of our shame and pain was at an end. All that remained was to say 'thank you'. That meant we had to rebuild France, taking account of its new limitations. The veil of illusion that had masked its real level of importance for fifty years had been torn at the very moment of Japanese capitulation. We men of forty have been saying for some time that France has, above all, to resign itself to playing a minor role. But we are so used to seeing it in major ones that we speak of it not as an ageing actress, but as a star who, for some moral reason, would have to agree for a time to pass incognito. However, a more austere younger generation is coming up behind us, a generation better suited to the new tasks, because it has known only a humiliated France. These young people are the men of the Peace. We were the men of a lost battle, of a war that is fizzling out. Will we be stragglers in the coming years; will we be lost souls? This war's end is also a little bit our own or, at least, it is the end of our youth.

We believed, on no evidential basis, that peace was the natural state and substance of the universe, that war was merely a temporary agitation of its surface. Today we recognize our error: the end of the war is quite simply the end of *this* war. The future has not yet begun: we no longer believe in the end of wars; and we are so used to the sound of arms, so benumbed by our injuries and hunger, that we no longer even quite manage wholly to wish for it. If someone told us tomorrow that a new conflict had broken out, we would say, with a resigned shrug, 'That's only to be expected.' Moreover, among the best of men, I find a silent consent to war, something like a commitment to the full tragedy of the human condition.

Pacifism still had in it the hope that one day, by patience and purity, we would bring about heaven on earth. The pacifists still believed it was humanity's birthright that things should not always go badly. Today, I see a lot of modest, thoughtful young people who lay claim to no rights, not even the right to hope. They loathe violence, but are not optimistic enough— are too practical—to dare to think we shall be able to do without it. I saw some who refused to report their precarious state of health to the recruiting board for fear of being declared unfit for service. 'I would look an idiot,' they would say, 'at the next war.' So it seems that this war, much more atrocious than the last, has left memories that are less bad. Perhaps because we believed for a long time that it was less stupid. It did not seem stupid to fight German imperialism, to resist the army of occupation.

It is only today that we see Mussolini, Hitler and Hiro Hito were merely petty tyrants. These rapacious, sanguinary powers that fell upon the democracies were, by a long way, the weakest nations. The petty tyrants are dead and fallen, their little feudal principalities of Germany, Italy and Japan are brought low. The world is simplified. Two giants stand alone and are not well disposed to one another. But it will be some time before this war reveals its true face. Its last moments served to remind us of human frailty. So, we are happy that it is ending, but not with the way it is ending.

A good number of Europeans would have preferred Japan to be invaded, crushed by naval bombardment. But the little bomb that can kill a hundred thousand at a stroke and which, tomorrow, will kill

two million, brings us up suddenly against our respon-
sibilities. The next time, the earth could be blown up:
that absurd end would leave forever in suspense the
problems that have been our concern for over ten
thousand years. No one would ever know whether humanity could have overcome racial hatred, whether it
would have found a solution to class struggles. When
one thinks of it, everything seems futile. And yet humanity had, one day, to come into possession of its
death. Up until now it had led a life that came to it
from who knows where and—since it lacked the
means to commit suicide—it didn't even have the
power to reject self-inflicted death.

Wars made little crater-shaped holes, quickly filled
in, among this compact mass of the living. Everyone
was safe in the crowd, protected from the antediluvian
nothingness by the generations of their ancestors,
from the future nothingness by the generations of
their descendants—always in the middle of time,
never at the extremes. And yet, here we are, back at
the millennium. Each morning, we shall be on the eve
of the end of time, on the eve of the day when our
honesty, courage and goodwill will no longer have any

71

meaning for anyone, and will perish, together with ill-will, spite and fear, no distinction remaining between them. After the death of God, the death of man is now announced.

From this point on, my freedom is purer: this act I commit today will have neither God nor man as its everlasting witness. I have to be, now and for all eternity, my own witness. I have to be moral on this booby-trapped earth because I want to be. And if the whole of humanity continues to live, it will do so not simply because it has been born but because it will have decided to prolong its life. There is no longer any *human species*. The community that has appointed itself guardian of the atom bomb stands above the realm of nature, being responsible now for its life and death. It will be necessary every day, every minute, for it to consent to live. This is what we are anxiously feeling today. 'But no,' you will say, 'we are quite simply at the mercy of a madman.' That is not true: the atom bomb isn't available to any old lunatic; that madman would have to be a Hitler and, as with the original Führer, we would all be responsible for the emergence of a new one. So, just as this war is coming to an end, we have come full circle. In each of us humanity discovers its potential death, takes responsibility for its life and death.

Should we give up the idea of building this peace, the most perilous of all, because we no longer believe in Peace, because our country has lost many of its powers, because the potential suicide of the earth taints our undertakings with a subtle nothingness? Quite the contrary. I can understand, but cannot condone, the sentiments of that young Russian woman, a naturalized French citizen since childhood, who wept on the day of victory, saying, 'I'm from a little country! I'm from a little country and I want to be from a big country that's genuinely victorious.' And yet she was Russian by birth: perhaps she was nostalgic for her country of origin. But what do we who were born in France have to say? To say this is our homeland is not much. Most importantly, it is vague.

France is our concrete situation, our opportunity and our lot in life. It is still—more than ever—within national frameworks that personal development takes place. Internationalism, which was a fine dream, is now just the stubborn illusion of a few Trotskyites.

What can we do, then? To deny the French community is to deny ourselves. And if we gamble on life, on our friends, on our person, we gamble on France, we commit ourselves to seeking to integrate it into this rough, tough world, into this mortally endangered humanity. We have also to gamble on the earth, even if one day it should be smashed to pieces. Simply because that is where we are.

God is dead. The 'sacred, inalienable rights' are dead and buried. The war is dead and with it have gone the justifications and alibis it offered to weak souls, the hopes of a gentle and just peace it kept alive in people's hearts. 'Up to now I lived in anxiety,' said Tristan Bernard when they came to arrest him. 'Now I shall live in hope.' On the day of Japanese surrender, we would be able to say precisely the opposite. No longer shall we read each morning in the newspapers the comforting news of a minor or major German defeat. The dailies will tell us of the rebirth of the military spirit in Germany, of civil war in China, of the diplomatic difficulties encountered by the Three, the Four or the Five. But we have to gamble. As it dies, the war leaves man naked and without illusions; he is

74

abandoned now to its own devices, having at last understood that he has only himself to rely on. This is
the only good piece of news that thin, ceremonious
burst of gunfire brought us the other afternoon.

Les Temps modernes, October 1945.

Notes

1   If one had to find an excuse, or at least an explanation, for 'collaboration', we should say that it too was
an effort to give France a future.

2   Marcel Déat (1894–1955): French Socialist who
drifted towards fascism, via what he termed 'neo-So-
cialism', in the late 1930s. In 1941, he founded the
fascistic Rassemblement National Populaire (PPF).
[Notes 2–19 are mine—Trans.]

3   Abel Bonnard (1883–1968): French Minister of Education under the Vichy regime and a member of
the Académie française; was a Maurrassian who
came to support Doriot's fascistic Parti Populaire
Française.

4   La Cagoule was the nickname of the so-called Or-
ganisation secrète d'action révolutionnaire, founded
in 1935 by Eugène Deloncle. Its members, the
Cagoulards, were united by fascistic leanings and a
taste for political violence.

5   Real name Jacques Talagrand (1908–88). An intellectual who wrote on social and artistic matters for publications of the extreme Right.

6   Jean Luchaire (1901–46): prominent collaborationist
editor of *Les Nouveaux Temps*. Condemned to death
for collaboration and executed.

7   Adrien Marquet (1885–1955): one time socialist
    mayor of Bordeaux; was Minister of the Interior
    under the Vichy regime for a brief period in 1940.

8   Jacques Doriot (1898–1945): former leading Commu-
    nist and founder of the Parti Populaire Français, one
    of France's larger authentically fascist movements.

9   Pierre Drieu la Rochelle (1893–1945): prominent fas-
    cist novelist and essayist.

10 Ramon Fernandez (1894–1944): fascist novelist and
    literary critic.

11 Alain Laubreaux (1899–1968): French fascist
    journalist.

12 A weekly newspaper, founded in 1930 under the ed-
    itorship of the historian Pierre Gaxotte, notorious
    after 1932 for its pro-fascist leanings.

13 Henri Béraud (1888–1958): leading French journalist
    who began with Leftist affiliations (he wrote, most
    notably, for *Le Canard enchainé*) but later drifted to-
    wards the far Right. He was condemned to death in
    1944 for 'intelligence with the enemy' but was par-
    doned by de Gaulle.

14 Founded in 1898, the Action française was France's
    leading monarchist organization. Its chief ideologues
    were Charles Maurras and Léon Daudet (son of the
    more famous Alphonse de Châteaubriant).

15 Alphonse de Châteaubriant (1877–1951): Goncourt-winning novelist and exuberant pro-Nazi ideologue.

16 Otto Abetz (1903–58): German Ambassador to Paris during the Second World War and a close friend of Jean Luchaire (see note 5).

17 Robert Brasillach (1909–45): prominent pro-fascist novelist and essayist.

18 Joseph Darnand (1897–1945): head of the notorious Vichy *Milice*. Executed for collaboration.

19 By a French tradition of obscure origin, when someone finds a double almond and shares it, the first of the two to shout 'Philippine' after midnight wins a gift from the other.

PART TWO

*individualism and conformism
in the united states*

How can you talk about a hundred and thirty-five million Americans? We would need to have lived in this
country for ten years and we shall be spending only six
weeks here. We are put down in cities where we pick
up a few details—yesterday Baltimore, today
Knoxville, the day after tomorrow New Orleans—
and then, after admiring the biggest factory or the
biggest bridge or the biggest dam in the world, we fly
off again, our heads full of facts and figures.

We shall have seen more steel and aluminium than
human beings. But can one speak about steel? As for
'impressions', they come as and when they please.

Some say, 'Keep to the facts!'

But what facts? The length of this shipyard in feet or the electric blue of the oxyhydrogen torch in the pale light of this shed? In choosing, I am already deciding what America is.

Others, by contrast, say, 'Step back and get some perspective on things!' But I distrust those perspectives that are already generalizations. So I've decided to convey my personal impressions and constructions, taking the responsibility on myself. Perhaps I've dreamed this America. I shall, at any rate, be honest with my dream: I shall set it out just as I dreamed it.

And today I would like to give you my impression of those two contradictory 'slogans' doing the rounds in Paris: 'the American is a conformist' and 'the American is an individualist'.

Like everyone else, I had heard tell of the famous American 'melting pot' which, at various critical temperatures, transforms a Pole, an Italian and a Finn into citizens of the United States. But I did not quite know what it meant.

Well, on the very day after I arrived I met a European in the process of 'melting'. In the main lobby of the Plaza Hotel I was introduced to a dark-haired man of quite modest stature who, like everyone here, talked with a slightly nasal twang, without visible movement of his lips or cheeks, who laughed with his mouth, but not with his eyes, and who expressed himself in a good, but heavily accented French, his speech sprinkled with barbarisms and Americanisms.

When I complimented him on his knowledge of our language, he replied with astonishment, 'But that's because I'm French.' He was born in Paris, has been living in American for only fifteen years and, before the war, went back to France every six months. Yet he is already half in the grip of America. His mother has never left Paris: when he speaks of *Paname* in deliberately vulgar tones he sounds much more like a Yankee wanting to show off his knowledge of Europe than an exiled Frenchman recalling his homeland. He feels obliged from time to time to cast roguish winks in my direction, saying 'Aha! New Orleans, fine women!' But, in so doing, he is conforming more to the

American's idea of the Frenchman than seeking collusion with a compatriot. 'Fine women', and he laughs, but in a forced way. Puritanism isn't far off and I feel a chill run down my spine.

I felt as though I were present at an Ovidian metamorphosis: the man's face was still too expressive, it retained that faintly annoying mimicry of intelligence by which you can recognize a French face anywhere. But he would soon be a tree or a rock. I wondered with some curiosity what powerful forces had to be brought into play to achieve such integrations and disintegrations so surely and swiftly.

Now, these forces are mild and persuasive. You have only to walk the streets, enter a shop or switch on a radio to encounter them, to feel their effect on you like a warm breath.

In America—at least the America I know—you are never alone in the street. The walls speak to you. To left and right of you there are posters, illuminated advertisements and enormous shop windows simply containing large boards with photomontages or tables of statistics. Here, you have a distraught woman leaning over to kiss an American soldier, there, a plane

84

dropping bombs on a village, and, beneath the picture, the words, 'Bibles, not bombs'. The nation walks with you. It proffers advice and commands. But it does so sotto voce and is careful to explain its orders in minute detail. There is no injunction that is not accompanied by a brief commentary or a justificatory image, whether in an advert for cosmetics (Today, more than ever, you have to be beautiful. Take care of your face for when *he* comes home: buy cream X.) or in propaganda for War Bonds.

I dined yesterday in a restaurant at Fontana, an artificial village built around a great dam in Tennessee.

All along the road leading to that dam, a road full of lorries, automobiles and pick-up trucks, a great hoarding conveys a parable in cartoon form on the subject of working together. Two donkeys roped together are trying to reach two piles of hay some distance apart. Each pulls on the rope in its own direction and they are half-strangling each other. Finally, they understand. They move together and begin merrily munching the first pile together. When they have eaten it, we see them starting out in unison towards the second.

Clearly, it was a deliberate decision to banish all commentary. The passers-by *have to* draw the conclusion *themselves*. No violence is done to them. On the contrary, the image is an appeal to their intelligence. They are obliged to interpret and understand it. It does not bludgeon them, as Nazi propaganda did with its garish posters. It remains low-key. It requires participation if it is to be deciphered. When they have understood, it is as though they had formed the idea themselves. They are already more than half convinced.

In the factories, they have put up loudspeakers everywhere. These are intended to combat the workers' isolation in their encounter with matter.

Walking through the immense naval dockyard near Baltimore, you first encounter that human dispersal, that great solitude of the workers so familiar to us in Europe. Masked men, bending over steel plates, spend all day working with their oxyhydrogen torches. But as soon as they put on their headphones, they can hear music. And the music is already guidance insinuating itself stealthily into them, it is already a guided dream. And then the music stops and they receive information about the war or their work.

When we left Fontana, the engineer who had so kindly taken us everywhere led us into a little glass room where a new wax disc was revolving, readied for the recording of our voices. He explained that all the visitors who had visited the dam had summed up their impressions at the microphone before they left. We were not about to refuse such a kind host. Those of us who knew English spoke and our words were recorded. The next day they would be broadcast in the dockyard, in the canteen and to all the houses in the village, and the workers would be encouraged to continue their good work, learning with pleasure of the excellent impression they had made on a group of foreigners.

Add to this the advice meted out by the radio and in the columns of the newspapers and, particularly, the activities of the countless voluntary organizations whose aims are almost always educational, and you will see that the American citizen is tightly hedged about.

But it would be an error to see this as an oppressive manoeuvre on the part of the government or big American capitalists.

The present government is, of course, at war. It is obliged, for purposes of war propaganda, to use such methods. Doubtless, too, one of its main concerns is education.

In Tennessee, for example, where the farmers ruined the soil by the repeated planting of maize, it is trying to teach them gradually to allow the soil to rest by varying their crops each year. To achieve its goal, it has combined gifts (low-cost electricity, free irrigation) with argument. But what we have here is a much more spontaneous and diffuse phenomenon.

This educative tendency really springs from the heart of the community. Every American is educated by other Americans and educates others in turn. All over New York, both in the schools and outside, there are courses in Americanization.

And they teach everything: sewing, cooking, even romance. There is a course in a New York school on how a girl should go about getting her boyfriend to marry her. In all this, it is not so much a question of training a human being as training a pure American. But Americans make no distinction between American reason and reason *tout court*. All the advice with which their route is studded is so perfectly motivated, so penetrating, that they feel themselves cradled by an immense solicitude that never leaves them helpless or alone.

I have met some of these 'modern' mothers who have never ordered their children to do anything without first persuading them to obey. They have acquired a more total, and perhaps more formidable, authority over them than if they had used threats and blows. In the same way, the American, whose reason and freedom are appealed to at every hour of the day, makes it a point of honour to do what he is asked. It is by acting like everyone else that he feels both most reasonable and most American; it is by displaying the greatest conformism that he feels most free.

So far as I can judge, the characteristics of the American nation are the opposite of those which Hitler gave to Germany and Maurras wanted to give to France.

For Hitler (or Maurras), an argument is good for Germany if, first of all, it is German. It is always suspect if it has any slight whiff of universality.

By contrast, it is the peculiar characteristic of the American that he regards his thought as universal. One can detect a Puritan influence here which I need not go into at this point. But there is, above all, this concrete, daily presence of a flesh-and-blood Reason, a Reason you can see. Most of the people I spoke to seemed to have a naïve, passionate faith in the virtues of Reason. One evening an American said to me, 'If international politics were carried on by reasonable, sane men, wouldn't war be abolished forever?' Some French people present pointed out that the matter was not so straightforward and he grew angry. 'All right,' he said, with indignant contempt, 'go and build graveyards!' I, for my part, said nothing. Discussion between us was not possible. I believe in evil and he does not.

It is this Rousseauesque optimism which distances the American from our standpoint where Nazi Germany is concerned. In order to accept the atrocities, he would have to accept that man can be wholly evil. 'Do you believe there are two Germanies?' an American doctor asked me. I replied that I did not.

'I understand,' he said. 'You can't think otherwise because France has suffered so much. But it's a pity.'

Machines play a part here. They too are universal izing factors. With mechanical objects, there is generally only one way to use them; the one indicated in the accompanying leaflet. The American uses his mechanical corkscrew, his fridge or his automobile at the same time as all the other Americans and in the same way. Besides, the object is not made to order. It is for anyone and will work for anyone, provided he knows how to use it properly.

So, when the American puts his nickel in the slot in the tram, the subway or the drinks machine, he feels like anyone. Not like an anonymous unit, but like a person who has divested himself of his individuality and elevated himself to the impersonality of the Universal.

It was this total freedom in conformism that struck me first. No city is freer than New York. You can do as you like there. Public opinion itself keeps order. The few Americans I met seemed conformist out of freedom, depersonalized by rationalism, and they identified universal Reason with their own particular Nation as part of a single creed.

But almost immediately I discovered their profound individualism. This combination of social conformism and individualism is perhaps what a Frenchman will have the greatest difficulty understanding. For us, individualism has retained the old, classical form of 'the individual's struggle against society and, particularly, against the state'. This is not what it means in America. First, the state was for a long time only an administrative body. For some years now, it has tended to play a different role, but this has not changed the Americans' feelings towards it. It is 'their' state, it is the expression of 'their' nation: they have a deep respect and a proprietary love for it.[1]

If you just walk about in New York for a few days, you cannot help but notice the profound link between American conformism and individuality. Taken lengthwise and from side to side, New York, laid flat, is the most conformist city in the world. If you except old Broadway, then from Washington Square not one street curves or runs diagonally. Some ten long parallel furrows run straight from the tip of Manhattan to the Harlem River. These are the avenues and they are crossed by hundreds of smaller furrows that are strictly perpendicular to them.

This grid pattern is New York: the streets are so alike that they have not been given names; like soldiers, they have merely been assigned a number.

But look up and everything changes. Viewed in terms of height, New York is the triumph of individualism. The buildings escape upwards from planning regulations. They have twenty-five, fifty-five or a hundred storeys; they are grey, brown, white, Moorish, medieval, renaissance or modern. On Lower Broadway they press up against each other, dwarfing tiny black churches, and then suddenly they spread out, leaving a gaping hole of light between them. Seen from Brooklyn, they seemed to me to have the solitude and nobility of the clumps of palm trees by the rivers in the Moroccan Souss: clumps of skyscrapers which the eye is always trying to bind together and which always come apart.

So American individualism seemed to me, initially, like a third dimension. In no sense is it opposed to conformism. Indeed, it presupposes it. But within conformism it is a new direction, upwards and downwards.

First there is the struggle for existence—and it is very harsh. Every individual wants to succeed—that is to say, to make money. But we should not see this as greed, nor even as a taste for luxury. It seems to me that in the USA, money is merely the necessary, but symbolic, token of success. You must succeed, because success proves your moral virtue and intelligence, and because it indicates that you enjoy divine protection.

And you must succeed because only then can you stand out from the crowd as a person. Take the American newspapers. Until you are a success, there is no point hoping that your articles will be published in the form in which you submitted them. They will be cut and pruned. But if you have a name that makes money, all that changes. What you write will go through without editing. You have acquired the right to be yourself.

It is the same in the theatre. A lady very well-versed in French literature and well-known in publishing circles asked me if I would like to have a play put on in the States. I replied that I would be happy to, if the directors were not, as I had been told, in the habit of reworking the scripts submitted to them. She seemed most surprised and said, 'If they don't do it, who will? What you wrote is meant to be read. But they have to work on it, so that it can be understood.'[2]

So, individualism in America is, above all, each person's passionate aspiration, in the struggle for existence, to the state of individual. There are individuals in America the way there are skyscrapers. There's Ford, there's Rockefeller, there's Hemingway, there's Roosevelt: they are models and examples.

In this sense, the office blocks are votive offerings to success. Behind the Statue of Liberty, they are like the statues of a man or an enterprise that have risen above the others. They are huge publicity ventures, built by individuals or groups to demonstrate their financial triumph. Their owners occupy only a small part of the premises and let out the rest. I was not mistaken, then, in taking them to symbolize New York individualism. They quite simply mark the fact that in the United States individuality is something to be achieved. It is no doubt for this reason that New Yorkers seemed to me so passionately attached to a free-market economy.

Yet everyone knows the power of the trusts in the USA, which represents, all in all, another form of command economy. But the New Yorker hasn't forgotten the day when a man could earn a fortune off his own bat. What he finds distasteful in the command economy is bureaucracy. So, rather paradoxically, this man who allows himself to be led so obediently by the nose in his public and private life is intransigent when it comes to his job. This he regards as the sphere of his independence, initiative and personal dignity.

For everything else, there are the 'associations'. In 1930, there were more than a hundred and fifty headquarters of associations and groups in Washington. I shall mention just one of them, the Foreign Policy Association.

On some seventeenth floor, 'over a cup of tea', we met some of those tall, grey-haired women, who have made up a majority in these associations since the war began; they are amiable but rather cold, and as intelligent as men. They told us how in 1917 a number of people, firmly convinced that the United States was entering the war without knowing anything of foreign affairs, had decided to devote their free time to providing the country with the information it lacked.

The organization has twenty-six thousand members today, with three hundred branches in the various states. It provides documentation to more than five hundred newspapers. Politicians consult its publications. It has, indeed, given up on informing the general public: it now informs the informers (scholars, teachers, priests and journalists). Every week it publishes a bulletin with a study of an international question and commentary on events in Washington and once a fortnight it sends documentation to the newspapers which they reprint in whole or in part.

Can one imagine in the France of 1939 an association of this kind providing Bonnet or Daladier with information and sending its bulletins to Maurras for inclusion in *Action française* and to Cachin for *L'Humanité*?

What struck me most forcefully were our hostess' last words: 'The point,' she said, 'is that we protect the individual. Outside of the associations a man is alone; in the associations he is a person; and he protects himself against each of them by belonging to several.' You can see the meaning of this individualism: the citizen must first fit into a structure and protect himself; he must enter into a social contract with other citizens of his own kind. And it is this smaller community that will confer upon him his individual function and personal worth. Within the association he will take initiatives, will be able to advocate a personal policy and, if he is able to, influence the collective orientation.

Just as the solitary individual arouses distrust in the USA, so this directed, hedged-in individualism is encouraged. This is illustrated, at quite another level, by the attempts made by leaders of industry to foster self-criticism among their staff.

When the worker is in a trade union, when government and managerial propaganda have sufficiently integrated him into the community, *then* he is asked to distinguish himself from the others and show initiative. On more than one occasion, at a factory entrance, we came across brightly coloured booths where improvements proposed by members of the workforce were displayed under glass, together with photographs of their inventors who frequently receive bonuses for their efforts.

I have said enough, I hope, to convey how the American citizen is subjected, from cradle to grave, to an intense force of organization and Americanization; how he is first depersonalized by a constant appeal to his reason, public-spiritedness and freedom; and how, when he is duly slotted into the nation by professional organizations and by the associations for moral edification and education, he suddenly recovers awareness of himself and his personal autonomy. He is then free to escape towards an almost Nietzschean individualism symbolized by the skyscrapers in the clear skies of New York. In any event, it is not individualism that is the basic element here, but conformism. Personality must be won: it is a social function or the affirmation of success.

Le Figaro, March 1945.

cities of america

The first few days I was lost. I had not adjusted to the skyscrapers, yet they did not amaze me. They did not seem like human constructions inhabited by men but, rather, like those dead parts of the cityscape, those rocks and hills that you find in cities built on rugged terrain and skirt around without even noticing. At the same time I was perpetually looking for something to hold my attention for a moment. Something I never found. A detail, a square perhaps, or a monument. I didn't yet know you have to look at the houses and streets here in bulk.

To learn to live in these cities and to love them as the Americans do, I had to fly over the vast deserts of the west and the south. In Europe, our towns are contiguous. They are immersed in a human countryside that has been worked over yard by yard. And then we are vaguely aware that there is, very far away across the sea, a mythical entity known as the desert. For the American, that myth is a daily reality. Between New Orleans and San Francisco we flew for hours over dry, red earth, studded with grey-green bushes. Suddenly a city welled up, a little grid on the ground, and then once again there was red earth, the savannah, the twisted rocks of the Grand Canyon and the snows of the Rockies.

After a few days of this, I came to see that an American city was, originally, a camp in the desert. People from some far-off place, drawn to the site by a mine, an oilfield or good agricultural land, arrived one fine day and settled there as quickly as they could in a clearing on the banks of a river. They built the essential organs, bank, city hall and church, then wooden bungalows by the hundreds. The road, if there was one, served as a spine; perpendicular to it, they traced out streets like vertebrae. The American towns that have this kind of centre parting are almost too numerous to count.

Nothing has changed since the days of the wagon trains. Each year towns are founded in the United States and they are founded by the same procedures.

Take Fontana in Tennessee, near one of the great TVA[N] dams. Twelve years ago, pine trees grew on the red soil of the mountain. As soon as they began to build the dam, they cut down the pine trees and three villages sprang from the soil: two white ones, with three thousand and five thousand inhabitants respectively, and a black one. The workers live there with their families. Four or five years ago, at the height of the works, the birth rate was running at one per day. Half the village has a lakeside air to it. The houses are timber-built with green roofs and have been built on piles to avoid the damp. The other half is made of collapsible dwellings, the so-called prefabricated houses. They too are built of timber; they are constructed some six hundred miles away and loaded onto lorries. When they arrive, it takes just a single team a single day to erect them. The smallest of them cost the employer two thousand dollars and he rents them to his workers at nineteen dollars a month (thirty-one dollars furnished). Inside, with their mass-produced furniture, central heating, electric lights and refrigerators, they are reminiscent of ship's cabins. Every inch of these little antiseptic rooms has been utilized: there are cupboards in the walls and drawers under the bed.

You leave, somewhat weighed down, with the sense of having seen the meticulous, small-scale reconstruction of a 1944 flat in a Year-3000 world. As soon as you set foot outside, you see hundreds of exactly identical dwellings, piled up, squashed against the earth, yet still, in their very shape, retaining a nomadic air of sorts. They look like a caravan scrapyard. The lakeside village and the caravan scrapyard stand facing each other on either side of a road that climbs into the pines. There you have an American town, or rather the matrix of an American town, with all its essential organs. At the bottom a dime store, higher up the clinic, and at the top a 'mixed' church, where they provide what may be termed a basic service, valid for all denominations.

The striking feature is the lightness and fragility of these buildings. The village is weightless. It seems barely to rest on the soil. It has not yet managed to leave a human imprint on this reddish earth and the dark woods. It is *temporary*. And it will, indeed, soon be on the road again. In two years' time, the dam will be finished, the workers will leave and the prefabricated houses will be dismantled and sent to reconstruct another Fontana around an oil-well in Texas or a cotton plantation in Georgia, under different skies and with new residents.

There is nothing exceptional about this roving village. In the USA, towns are born the way they die: in one day. The Americans make no complaint: the main thing for them is to be able to take their homes with them. These 'homes' are the sets of objects, furnishings, photographs and souvenirs that belong to them, that reflect back their image and form the living inner landscape of their dwellings. They are their *Penates* and, like Aeneas, they haul them about everywhere.

The 'house' is the shell: they abandon it on the slightest pretext.

We have workers' settlements in France, but they are sedentary affairs and will never become real cities. They are, rather, the artificial product of neighbouring townships. In America, just as every citizen can in theory become president, so every Fontana can become a Denver or a Minneapolis: it just takes a little luck. Conversely, Denver and Minneapolis are Fontanas that have struck it lucky. To take just one example: in 1905, the population of Detroit was just three hundred thousand. Today, it is one million.

The inhabitants are perfectly aware of this luck. In their films and books they like to recall the time when their city was merely an encampment. And that is why they pass so easily from city to encampment: they make no distinction between the two. Detroit and Minneapolis, Knoxville and Memphis were *born temporary* and have remained so. They will doubtless never take to the road again on the back of a lorry. But they remain at melting point; they have never reached an internal solidifying temperature.

What for us would merely be a change of situation is for an American the occasion of a real break with his past. There were many who, when going off to war, sold off their apartments and everything else, even their suits: what point was there in keeping things that would be out of fashion by the time they returned? Soldiers' wives frequently adopt a reduced style of life and move to live more modestly in another part of town. Sadness and faithfulness to the absent soldier are marked by moving house.

Fluctuations in American fortunes are also marked by changes of neighbourhood. It is the rule in the United States for the fashionable areas of town to slide from the centre to the periphery. After five years, the centre is 'decayed'. If you walk around its dirty streets, you will come upon apartment buildings going to rack and ruin, but retaining an air of pretension beneath their filth; you will find complicated architecture—one-storey wooden-framed houses with entrances formed by peristyles supported by columns, Gothic chalets, 'colonial' houses and the like. They were once aristocratic residences; now the poor live there. There are Graeco-Roman temples in Chicago's grim Negro district. They still look good from the outside, but, inside, twelve lice- and rat-infested Negro families are crowded into five or six rooms.

At the same time, changes are continually being made. A block is purchased so that it can be demolished and a bigger block put up on the same site; after five years, it is sold to a developer who tears it down to build a third one. As a result, American cities are moving landscapes, whereas our cities are our protective shells.

Only a very old French person would be able to say what I heard a forty-year-old American say yesterday in Chicago: 'When I was young, this area here was all lake. But they filled in this part of the lake and built on it.' And this morning a thirty-five-year-old lawyer, showing me round the Negro district, said: 'I was born here. It was a white area then. You would not have seen a black person, except for servants. Today the whites have gone and a quarter of a million Negroes are crowded into their houses.'

Mr Verdier, who owns the large 'City of Paris' department store in San Francisco, saw the earthquake and the fire that destroyed three-quarters of the city. He was a young man, then, but he still remembers the disaster perfectly. He watched as the city was rebuilt— in 1913 it still had an Asiatic look to it—and then as it was rapidly Americanized. He has, then, superimposed memories of three San Franciscos.

We Europeans change in changeless cities and our houses and neighbourhoods outlive us. American cities change faster than their residents and it is the residents who outlive the cities.

We are, in fact, visiting the USA in wartime. The frantic liveliness of American cities has suddenly been petrified: there is no more building; hardly anyone moves house. But this stagnation is entirely temporary. The cities have come to a standstill, like a dancer on the screen whose leg stays in the air when the film stops. Everywhere you feel the sap rising that will make them burst into life again as soon as the war ends.

To begin with, there are some urgent problems. For example, the black district of Chicago has to be rebuilt. The government had set about the work before Pearl Harbor, but the buildings it put up can barely house seven thousand, and there are two hundred and fifty thousand to be accommodated. Then the industrialists want to expand and transform their factories: the famous Chicago meatyards are going to be completely modernized.

Lastly, the average American is obsessed with the image of the 'modern house', which is widely advertised and which will, we are told, be a hundred times more comfortable than today's dwellings. The construction of such homes in massive quantities definitely forms part of the 'industrial conversion' projects that are springing up almost everywhere at the moment.

After the war, America will certainly be seized with a real construction fever. The American looks on his city today with objectivity. It does not occur to him to find it ugly, but he finds it decidedly old. If it were even older, as ours are, he could find a social past in it, a tradition. We generally live in our grandfathers' dwellings. Our streets reflect the customs of bygone centuries; they tend to sift out the present a little and nothing of what goes on in the rue Montorgueil or the rue du Pot-de-Fer is entirely of the present. But at thirty years of age, the Americans live in houses that were built when they were twenty.

These houses, too young to look *old*, seem merely outmoded to them. They lag behind their other tools—the cars they can trade in every two years, the refrigerators, the radio sets. That is why they see their cities rationally, without empty sentimentality. They are somewhat attached to them, the way you become attached to a car, but they see them first and foremost as instruments which they will unhesitatingly exchange for handier ones.

For us, a city is, first and foremost, a past. For them, it is mainly a future. What they like in it is everything it has not yet become, everything it can be.

What are the European's impressions when he lands in an American city? First, he thinks he has been 'had'. All the talk has been of skyscrapers, and New York and Chicago have been presented to him as 'cities standing tall'. Now, his first feeling is, on the contrary, that the average height of an American city is very appreciably less than that of a French one. The immense majority of houses are of no more than two storeys. Even in the very big cities, the five-storey block is the exception.

Then he is struck by the lightness of the materials used. In the USA, stone is hardly ever used. The sky-scrapers have a metal framework encased in concrete; the other buildings are of brick or timber. Even in the richest cities and the smartest neighbourhoods, one frequently finds timber-built houses. The fine colonial residences of New Orleans are built of wood, as are the pretty chalets where the Hollywood directors live and the 'Californian style' cottages of San Francisco. Everywhere you find groups of timber-built houses crushed between two twenty-storey blocks.

The brick houses are the colour of dried blood or, by contrast, daubed and smeared with green, bright yellow or harsh white.[4] In most of the cities they have no sloping roofs; they are cubes or rectangular parallelepipeds with severely flat facades. All these dwellings, hastily built and deliberately made to be hastily demolished, are singularly akin, as we have seen, to the 'pre-fabricated houses' of Fontana.

The lightness of these jerry-built constructions, their garish colours alternating with the dark red of the bricks, and the extraordinary variety of decoration on them, though it fails to conceal the uniformity of their pattern, all give a feeling, even in the middle of the city, of walking in the suburbs of a seaside resort. One might be in Trouville, Cabourg or La Baule. Only ephemeral seaside chalets, with their fragility and pretentious architecture, can give an idea of American apartment houses to those French readers who have never seen the US.

I should also add, to complete the impression, that one thinks at times, too, of the buildings put up for an exposition, but old, dirty ones, such as those that outlive by ten years the solemn occasion that brought them into being. For these shanties soon grow dirty, particularly in industrial areas.

Chicago, blackened by its smoke, made gloomy by the fogs of Lake Michigan, is a dark, grim red. Pittsburgh is even darker. And nothing is more striking at first than the contrast between the formidable power and inexhaustible abundance of what is called the 'American colossus' and the puny insignificance of the little houses that line the widest roads in the world. But, when one thinks of it, there is nothing that underlines better the fact that America is unfinished, that its ideas and plans, its social structure and cities have but a strictly provisional reality.

These cities laid out straight as a die bear not the slightest hint of organization. Many of them have the rudimentary structure of polyparies. Los Angeles, in particular, looks like a large earthworm you could cut into twenty sections without killing it. Moving through that enormous conurbation, which is probably the largest in the world, you come in succession to twenty juxtaposed cities, each strictly identical to the next, each with its poor district, its shopping streets, its nightclubs and its smart suburb; you get the impression that a medium-sized urban centre has made twenty copies of itself by scissiparous reproduction.[5]

This juxtaposition is the rule in America, where neighbourhoods are tacked on to each other as the prosperity of one region brings in new immigrants. You pass without transition from a poverty-stricken street to an aristocratic avenue. An esplanade lined with sky-scrapers, museums and public monuments and adorned with lawns and trees comes to a sudden halt above a smoky station. And it is not unusual to find a wasteland of scrawny little kitchen gardens beneath the tallest apartment blocks on some aristocratic avenue.

The fact is that the past, in these fast-moving cities—which are not built to grow old but which, like modern armies, advance by encircling islets of resist-ance they cannot destroy—does not manifest itself, as it does with us, in *monuments*, but in *survivals*. The wooden bridge in Chicago that crosses a canal a stone's throw from the world's highest skyscrapers is a survival. The elevated railways that rattle noisily through the streets of downtown Chicago and New York, supported by great iron pillars and cross-girders, almost touching the housefronts on either side, are survivals. They are quite simply there because there hasn't been time to pull them down; they are an indication of work still to be done.

The same disorder repeats itself in each individual vista. Nowhere else have I seen so many areas of wasteland. Admittedly, they have a precise function: they serve as car parks. But that doesn't mean they break up the alignment of the streets any less sharply. All of a sudden, it seems a bomb has dropped on three or four houses, reducing them to rubble, which has just been cleared away: this is a 'car park', two hundred square metres of bare earth with perhaps an advertising poster on a large hoarding as its sole ornamentation. Suddenly the city seems unfinished, badly put together. Equally suddenly, you are back in the desert and those great empty sites that were so striking at Fontana.

I recall the following landscape in Los Angeles: in the middle of the city two modern apartment blocks, two white cubes, frame an area of waste ground full of potholes—a car park. There are some automobiles parked there, seemingly abandoned. A palm tree grows like a weed between the cars. At the bottom, a steep

grassy hill, somewhat akin to those mounds of our for
tifications where we dump household waste. At the top
of the mound, a wooden house. Not far below, a string
is tied between two little trees, with multi-coloured
washing hung out to dry on it. Walk around the blocks
and the hill disappears; the other side of it has been
faced with stone, asphalted and covered with tarmac
roads; a magnificent tunnel runs through it.

What is particularly striking about American cities
is the disorder in their height. The brick houses are
of unequal size. A walk in Detroit produced the following succession, which I noted down randomly: one
storey, two storeys, one storey, one storey, three
storeys. You will find the same pattern at the other
end of the country, in Albuquerque or San Antonio.
Above and behind this irregular crenellation, you see
buildings of all shapes and sizes: long, flat cases or
fat, thirty-storey boxes of thirty or forty windows to
a storey. As soon as there's a little fog, the colours
vanish. Volumes alone remain—every variety of poly-
hedron. Between them lie enormous spaces, waste-
lands cut out of the sky.

In New York, and even in Chicago, the sky-scraper is on home ground. It imposes a new order on the city. But everywhere else it is out of place. The eye can establish no unity between these great bean-poles and the little houses that run along the ground. It searches, despite itself, for that skyline so well known in European cities, but it cannot find it. This is why the European initially has the sense of moving, not through a city, but through a jumble of rocks that looks like a city—not unlike Montpellier-le-Vieux.[6]

But he is also wrong to visit American cities the way you visit Paris or Venice. They are not meant for that. Streets here don't have the same meaning as they do with us. In Europe, a street is halfway between a major road and a covered 'public place'. It is on the same level as the cafe, as is proved by the 'terraces' that sprout on our pavements on fine days. So, its appearance changes more than a hundred times a day, since the crowd that throngs it changes and in Europe human beings are its chief component. The American street is a section of main road. It sometimes stretches over several miles. It does not encourage you to walk. Our streets are oblique and tortuous, full of recesses and secrets. The American street is a straight line; it yields itself immediately to the gaze and lacks mystery. Wherever you are, you can see from one end of it to the other. Moreover, in American cities the distances are too great to move around on foot. In most of them you travel almost exclusively by car, bus or subway train. Going from subway to escalator, escalator to taxi, taxi to bus and then again into the subway and a lift, I have sometimes travelled from one appointment to another like a parcel, never setting one foot in front of the other.

In some cities I found the pavements were genuinely atrophied. In Los Angeles, for example, on La Cinega, which is lined with bars, theatres, restaurants, antique shops and private residences, they are now scarcely more than the paths the guests and clients take to cross from the roadway into the building. Lawns have been laid between the facades and the roadway of this luxurious avenue. I followed a narrow path between these lawns for some time without encountering a living soul, while cars sped along the road to my right. All the animation of the street had found refuge on the roadway.

117

In New York and Chicago there are no neighbourhoods, but there is a neighbourhood life. The American does not know his city. Ten blocks from home, he is lost. This does not mean there are no crowds in the shopping streets. But it is a crowd that does not linger. People do their shopping or come out of the subway and go to their offices.

Only very rarely would I see a few Negroes daydreaming at a shop window.

Despite all this, you soon come to like American cities. Admittedly, they do all look alike. And it is disappointing to find, when you arrive in Wichita, St Louis, Albuquerque or Memphis, that hidden behind these magnificent, promising names is the same standard city with its checkerboard street pattern, the same red and green lights regulating the traffic and the same provincial air. But you gradually learn to tell one from the other. Chicago, noble and grim, red as the blood that streams through its slaughterhouses, with its canals, the grey water of Lake Michigan and its streets crushed between lumpish, mighty blocks is not a bit like San Francisco, that airy, briny city, sweeping down to the sea like an amphitheatre.

And then you end up liking their common element, the sense of the temporary. We are rather stifled in our fine, closed, chock-full cities. Our streets, winding and oblique, stumble into walls and houses. Once inside the city, you can no longer see beyond it. In America, these long straight unobstructed streets lead your gaze out of the city, as canals might do. Wherever you are, you see mountains or fields or the sea at the end of them.

Temporary and frail, formless and unfinished, these cities are haunted by the presence of the immense geographical space around them. Precisely because their boulevards are roads, they seem always to be staging-posts on a route. They are not oppressive, they never shut you in. Nothing in them is definitive or arrested. From the first glance, you feel your contact with these cities is a temporary one: either you will leave them or they will change around you.

But let us not exaggerate. In these same cities we have experienced American provincial Sundays—Sundays more oppressive than anywhere else on earth; we have seen the 'colonial style' suburban hostelries where, sitting in silence to the strains of an electric organ, middle-class families eat prawn cocktails and turkey in a sweet sauce at two dollars a head. We must not forget the dense layer of boredom that weighs upon America.

But these lightweight cities, still so like Fontana and the encampments of the Far West, show the other side of the US—its freedom. Everyone is free here, not to criticize or to reform how things are done, but to flee from it and go off into the desert or to some other town. The cities are open. They are open to the world and to the future. That is what gives them all an air of adventure; and, in their disorder and even ugliness, a kind of touching beauty.

Le Figaro, April 1945.

new york, colonial city

I knew I would love New York, but I thought I would be able to love it straight away, as I had loved the red bricks of Venice at first sight or the solid, sombre houses of London. I didn't know that for the European fresh off the plane, there is a 'New York sickness', akin to sea sickness, air sickness or altitude sickness.

An official coach had taken me from La Guardia airport to the Plaza Hotel at midnight. I had pressed my face against the window, but I could see only red and green lights and obscure buildings. The following day, without any transition, I found myself at the corner of Fifty-Eighth Street and Fifth Avenue. I took a long walk beneath an icy sky. It was a forlorn January Sunday in 1945 and I was looking for New York and couldn't find it. It was as though it drew back from me, like a ghost town, as I advanced along an avenue that seemed coldly mediocre and unoriginal. What I was looking for was, no doubt, a European city.

We Europeans live by the myth of the city we forged in the nineteenth century. The Americans' myths are not ours and the American city isn't our city. It hasn't the same nature or the same functions. In Spain, Italy, Germany or France, we find round cities originally encircled by ramparts, designed not only to protect the inhabitants from enemy invasion, but also to conceal from them the inexorable presence of nature. These cities are, moreover, divided into similarly rounded, closed districts. The tangle of jumbled houses weighs heavily on the ground. They seem to have a natural tendency to grow closer to each other—so much so that, from time to time, we have to take an axe to them to clear new paths, as you might in virgin forests. Streets run into other streets. They are closed at each end and do not seem to lead out of the city. Inside them, you go round in circles. They are more than mere arteries. each one is a social milieu. These are streets where you stop, meet people, drink, eat and linger. On Sundays, you dress up and take a stroll simply for the pleasure of greeting friends, of seeing and being seen. It is these streets that inspired Jules Romains' 'unanimism'. They are alive with a communal spirit that changes each hour of the day.

So, my short-sighted European eyes, venturing slowly and intently, strove in vain to find something to arrest them. Something, anything—a row of houses suddenly barring the way, a street corner or some old house bearing the patina of age. But to no avail. New York is a city for the long-sighted: you can 'focus' only at infinity. My gaze met nothing but space. It slid over blocks of identical houses, there being nothing to arrest it on its journey to the indistinctness of the horizon.

Céline called New York 'a vertical city'. This is true, but it seemed to me first a lengthways one. The traffic, at a standstill in the side streets, enjoys every possible privilege in the avenues, where it flows uninterrupted. How often the taxi-drivers, who are happy to take passengers north or south, refuse point blank to load up for east or west! The lateral streets have barely any other function than to mark the boundaries of the blocks between the avenues. The avenues cut through them and push them aside as they themselves rush on towards the north. It was for this reason, naïve tourist that I was, that I looked long and fruitlessly for distinct 'neighbourhoods'. In France, our urban clusters surround and protect us. The rich neighbourhood protects the rich from the poor; the poor neighbourhood keeps us from the disdain of the rich; in the same way, the entire city protects us from nature.

In New York, where the main thoroughfares are parallel avenues, I was unable, except in Lower Broadway, to find neighbourhoods. I could find only atmospheres—gaseous masses stretching out longitudinally, with nothing to mark their beginning or their end. Gradually, I learned to recognize the atmosphere of Third Avenue, where, without even knowing each other, people meet, smile and chat in the shade of the noisy elevated railway; and that Irish bar where a German, passing by my table, stopped for a moment to say: 'You're French? I'm a Boche'; the reassuring comfort of the stores on Lexington Avenue; the staid elegance of Park Avenue; the cold luxury and stuc-

coed impassiveness of Fifth Avenue; the merry frivol
ity of Sixth and Seventh; the 'food fair' of Ninth and
the no man's land of Tenth. Each avenue enwraps the
neighbouring streets in its atmosphere, but a block
away you suddenly plunge into another world. Not far
from the thrilling silence of Park Avenue, home to the
limousines of the powerful, I find myself on First Avenue, where the earth permanently shakes beneath the
weight of passing trucks. How can I feel safe on one
of these interminable north–south trajectories when,
a few feet away to east or west, other longitudinal
worlds lie in wait for me? Behind the Waldorf Astoria
and the white and blue canopies of the 'elegant' buildings, I glimpse the 'Elevated', which carries with it
something of the poverty of the Bowery.

The whole of New York is striped in this way
with parallel, non-communicating meanings. These
long lines, running straight as a die, suddenly gave me
a sense of space. Our European cities are built to protect us against this: the houses cluster together there
like sheep. But space runs through New York, animat-
ing and dilating it. Space, the great empty space of the
steppes and the pampas, runs in its veins like a

draught of cold air, separating those who live on the right from those who live on the left. In Boston, an American friend showing me round the smart neighbourhoods, pointed to the left of the street and said: 'This is where the "nice" people live.' And, pointing to the right, he added ironically, 'No one's ever found out who lives there.' It is the same in New York: between the two sides of a street, there is the whole of space.

New York is halfway between a city for pedestrians and a city for cars. You don't go for a walk in New York, you move through it; it is a city in motion. If I walk quickly, I feel at ease there. If I stop, I get flustered and wonder, 'Why am I on this street rather than on one of the hundreds of others like it?' Why in front of this drugstore, this branch of Schrafft's or Woolworth's, rather than any other one of the thousands like this?

And suddenly pure space appears. I imagine that a triangle, were it to acquire consciousness of its position in space, would be terror-stricken to learn of the rigour of its defining coordinates, and at the same time to discover that it is simply any old triangle, just anywhere. You never get lost in New York. You can see at a glance where you are: you are on the East Side, for example, at the corner of Fifty-Second Street and Lexington. But this spatial precision is not accompanied by any emotional exactitude. Amid the numerical anonymity of streets and avenues, I am simply anyone, anywhere. Wherever I am, my position is established in terms of longitude and latitude. But there is no valid reason to justify my presence at one spot rather than at another, since one place is so like another. I am never astray, but always lost.

Am I lost in a city or in nature? New York affords no protection from the violence of nature. It is a city open to the skies. The storms flood its streets that are so wide and take so long to cross when it rains. The hurricanes, announced solemnly on the radio like declarations of war, shake the brick houses and rock the skyscrapers. In summer, the air shimmers between the buildings. In winter, the city drowns as though you were in some Parisian suburb with the Seine overflowing, but here it is merely the snow melting.

Nature weighs so heavily on New York that this most modern of cities is also the dirtiest. From my window I can see the wind whipping up heavy muddy litter, which flits around on the pavement. Going out, I walk in blackish snow, a kind of puffy crust of the same hue as the sidewalk, as though that itself were buckling. From the end of May, the heat descends on the city like an atomic bomb. It is evil. People go up to each other and say: 'It's murder!' Millions of fleeing city-dwellers take to the trains, leaving damp marks on the seats when they get off, like snails. It isn't the city they are fleeing, but nature. Even in the depths of my apartment I suffer the depredations of a hostile, muffled, mysterious nature. I have the impression of camping in a jungle teeming with insects. There is the moaning of the wind, the electric shocks I get each time I touch a doorknob or shake a friend's hand, the cockroaches running round my kitchen, the elevators that make my stomach heave, the inextinguishable thirst that rages from morning to night. New York is a colonial city, a camp site. All the hostility and cruelty of nature are present in this city, the most prodigious monument humanity has ever raised to itself. It is a light city; its apparent weightlessness surprises most Europeans. In this immense, malevolent space, this desert of rock that brooks no vegetation, they have built thousands of houses out of brick, wood or rein forced concrete, all of which seem about to fly away.

I love New York. I have learned to love it. I have got used to its massive clumps of buildings, its long vistas. My eyes no longer linger over the facades searching for one that might, by some remote chance, not be just like all the others. They rove immediately to the horizon, looking for blocks lost in fog, which are now mere volumes, merely the austere framing of the sky. When you know how to look at the two rows of buildings that line any major thoroughfare like cliffs, you get your reward: their mission is accomplished at the far end of the avenue in simple harmonious lines; a scrap of sky floats between them.

New York reveals itself only at a particular height, a particular distance, a particular speed. These are not the height, the distance or the speed of the pedestrian. The city is strikingly like the great Andalusian plains—monotonous when you pass through on foot, superb and varying when crossed by car.

I have learned to love its sky. In the low-roofed cities of Europe, the sky crawls along the ground and

129

seems tamed. The beauty of the New York sky comes from its being raised so far above our heads by the skyscrapers. Pure and lonely as a wild beast, it mounts guard and stands watch over the city. And it isn't just a local protection: you feel that it stretches right out over the whole of America; it is the whole world's sky.

I have learned to love Manhattan's avenues. They are not sombre little walkways enclosed by houses, but national highways. As soon as you set foot in one of them you realize it has to go on as far as Boston or Chicago. Its vanishing point lies beyond the city and the eye can almost follow it out into the countryside. A wild sky above great parallel rails—that, first and foremost, is New York. In the heart of the city, you are in the heart of nature.

I had to get used to it, but now that I have, nowhere do I feel freer than amid the crowds of New York. This light, ephemeral city, which every morning and evening, beneath the curious rays of the sun, seems a mere juxtaposition of rectangular parallelepipeds, never oppresses or depresses. You can feel the anguish of solitude here, but not of prostration.

In Europe we cleave to a neighbourhood, a block of houses or a street corner, and we are no longer free. But hardly have you plunged into New York than you live entirely on its scale. You can look over it in the evening from up on the Queensboro Bridge, in the morning from New Jersey or at noon from the seventy-seventh floor of the Rockefeller Center, but you will never be captivated by any of its streets because none has a distinctive beauty all its own. Beauty is present in each of them, just as nature and the sky of the whole of America are present in them. Nowhere will you form a better sense of the simultaneity of human lives.

New York moves us Europeans despite its austerity. We have, admittedly, learned to love our old cities, but what touches us in them is a Roman wall forming part of the facade of an inn, a house where Cervantes lived, the Place des Vosges or the town hall at Rouen. We love museum-cities—and all our cities are a little like museums where we wander amid our ancestors' dwellings. New York isn't a museum-city. Yet for Frenchmen of my generation it already possesses the melancholy of the past. When we were twenty—

around 1925—we heard about the skyscrapers. For us they symbolized the fabulous prosperity of America. We discovered them with stupefaction in the movies. They were the architecture of the future, just as cinema was the art of the future and jazz the music of the future. Today we know all about jazz: it is more a music of the past than of the future. It is a popular black music, capable of limited development, but in gentle decline. It has had its day. And the talkies have not fulfilled the promise of the silents: Hollywood moulders on in a rut.

The war clearly revealed to the Americans that America is the world's greatest power. But the age of easy living is over: many economists fear a new recession. Hence, no skyscrapers are being built now. It seems they are too difficult to let.

To the man who strolled through New York before 1930, the high-rise buildings towering over the city were the first signs of an architecture destined to radiate over the entire country. Skyscrapers then were living things. Today, for a Frenchman arriving from Europe, they are already mere historical monuments, witnesses to a bygone age. They still rise up into the sky but my spirit does not soar with them, and the New Yorkers pass by at their feet without so much as a glance. I cannot think of them without melancholy: they speak of an age when we thought the war to end; war had just finished, an age when we believed in peace. They are already a little run-down: tomorrow, perhaps, they will be demolished. At any rate, to build them took a faith we no longer possess.

I walk between little brick houses the colour of dried blood. They are younger than Europe's houses, but their fragility makes them seem much older. I see in the distance the Empire State and Chrysler Buildings pointing vainly to the sky and it suddenly occurs to me that New York is on the point of acquiring a history and that it already has its ruins.

That is enough to soften somewhat the edges of the harshest city in the world.

Town and Country, May 1946.

usa: presentation

Everything has been said about the US. But once a
person has crossed the Atlantic he can no longer be
satisfied with even the most perceptive of books. Not
that he doesn't believe their message. But his commitment to it remains abstract. When a friend claims to
explain our character and fathom our intentions, when
he relates each of our actions to principles, prejudices,
beliefs and a worldview that are, in his view, our own,
we hear him out uneasily, without being able to either
deny what he says or entirely accept it. Perhaps the
construction is true, but true in what sense? The intimate warmth, the life, is lacking, as is that unpre-
dictability one always represents for oneself and that

134

weary familiarity also, and that decision to come to terms with—or run from—oneself and the endless deliberations and the perpetual invention of what one is, and the vow to be *this* and not something else: in a word, freedom.

In a similar way, when we in Europe are presented with a careful arrangement of the notions of melting-pot, puritanism, realism, optimism, etc., which we are told are the key to the American character, we feel a certain intellectual satisfaction and believe that it must indeed be that way. But when we walk in New York on Third, Sixth or Tenth Avenue at that hour of the evening that Leonardo saw as lending greater gentleness to the human countenance, we encounter the most moving faces in the world, faces uncertain and questing, assiduous, full of a wide-eyed good faith, with eyes that call out to us, and we know that the finest constructions will be of little use. They will enable us to understand the system, but not the people.

The system is a great external apparatus, an implacable machine we might call the objective spirit of the US and which, over there, they call 'Americanism'. It is a complex monster of myths, values, recipes, slogans, figures and rites. But we should not believe it has been deposited in the head of every American the way Descartes' God deposited his primary notions in the human mind. We should not believe it is 'refracted' into brains and hearts, at every moment determining affections or thoughts that are its rigorous expression. It is, in fact, outside them; it is *presented* to the citizens. The cleverest propaganda presents it to them incessantly, but it only ever presents it to them: it is not *it* that is in *them*, but *they* who are in *it*. They battle against it or accept it; they stifle in it or transcend it; they suffer it or repeatedly reinvent it anew; they give in to it or make furious efforts to escape it. In any event, *it* remains external to them, transcendent, for they are human beings and *it* is a thing.

There are the great myths—the myths of happiness, progress, freedom and triumphant motherhood—the realism and the optimism; and then there are the Americans who are nothing at first, who grow up between these colossal statues and make out as best they can amongst them. There is the myth of happiness; there are these bewitching slogans that tell you to be happy as quickly as possible; there are the films with 'happy endings' which, every evening, present exhausted crowds with a rose-tinted view of life; there is that language loaded with optimistic, carefree expressions—'have a good time', 'enjoy', 'life is fun', etc. And then there are these people who are haunted, even in the most conformist bliss, by an obscure, nameless malaise, these people who are tragic for fear of being so, from that total absence of the tragic in them and around them.

There is this community that prides itself on being the least 'historic' in the world; on never complicating its problems with inherited custom and acquired rights; on facing up, as a blank sheet, to a blank future where anything is possible. And then there are the blind stumblings of so many lost sheep who are trying to find sustenance in a tradition, a folklore. There are those films that write American history for the masses and which, for want of being able to serve up a Kentucky Joan of Arc or a Kansas Charlemagne, thrill those masses with the story of Al Jolson, jazz singer, or the composer George Gershwin. There is the Monroe Doctrine, isolationism and the contempt for Europe. And then there is every American's sentimental attachment to his country of origin and the intellectuals' inferiority complex towards the culture of the old Continent: the critics who say, 'How can you admire our novelists when you have Flaubert?' and the painters who say, 'I'll never be able to paint so long as I stay in the US.' There is the slow, barely perceptible effort of a whole nation to seize hold of universal history and assimilate it as its heritage. There is the myth of equality and there is 'segregation' and those great hotels in the Atlantic beach resorts with signs outside saying 'No Jews and no dogs', the Connecticut lakes where Jews are forbidden to bathe and the table of racial ranks where the lowest place is assigned to the Slavs and the highest to the Dutch immigrants who go back to 1680. There is the myth of freedom and the dictatorship of public opinion, the myth of economic liberalism and those big companies that extend over a whole continent which ultimately belong to no one and where everyone, from top to bottom, works like a functionary in a state industry. There is the legalistic mania that leads each citizen to call for new laws at every turn and the secret anarchy, that 'law of the heart', that leads them to find a loophole in every one.

There is the smiling belief in progress and the deep discouragement and pessimism of the intellectuals, who think that action is impossible. There is the respect for science and industry, the positivism, the fanatical love of gadgetry, and there is the dark humour of the *New Yorker* that bitterly mocks mechanical civilization and those hundred million Americans who beguile their immense need for the fantastic by reading the improbable adventures of Superman, Wonderwoman and Mandrake the Magician in the comic books.

There are the thousand taboos proscribing sex outside marriage, and then there are the carpets of used condoms in the backyards of the co-ed colleges, the cars parked by the road sides every evening with their lights off, all the men and women who drink before making love, so that they can sin while drunk and not remember it. There are the neat, tidy houses, the apartments all done out in white, with radio, rocking-chair and pipe in the pipe-box—veritable paradises. And then there are the tenants of these apartments who, after dinner, walk out on rocking-chair, radio, wife, pipe and children and drink themselves into a stupor alone in the bar opposite. Perhaps nowhere will

139

you find such a discrepancy between men and myths, between life and the collective representation of life. An American once said to me in Berne, 'The truth is that each of us has a nagging fear of being less American than his neighbour.' I accept this explanation. It shows that Americanism isn't a mere myth dinned into people's heads by artful propaganda, but that every American tentatively reinvents it at every moment, that it is both a grand external form, which stands at the entry to the port of New York, opposite the Statue of Liberty, and the daily product of uneasy freedoms. There is a sense of anxiety about Americanism in the American; there is an ambivalence to his anxiety, as though he were asking himself both: 'Am I American enough?' and 'How can I escape Americanism?' A human being in America is a certain simultaneous answer to these two questions; and each human being must find his answers alone.

The reader will be very disappointed if he expects to find an exhaustive study of America's problems here.[7] There is no point my saying what is lacking: in a sense, almost everything. But our aim has been to show human beings. Of all these articles, only six were written by Europeans; only six present the situation 'objectively'. In all the others, the authors speak of themselves and their condition: it is blacks who write about the Negroes,[8] an American psychoanalyst who writes about psychoanalysis, a New Yorker who writes of Broadway and the life story of Mrs Gertrude R. is told by that lady's very own daughter. So each of these testimonies is impassioned: Wylie's 'Mom' is an explosion of rage; we do not publish it with any documentary intent, but as typical of certain violent—and unjust—reactions of Americans to their own myths. They are also acts: 'Black Metropolis' isn't comparable to the studies of USA's Negro problem by Myrdal, the European; it is an attempt by intelligent, educated Negroes to raise the level of their race. The presentation of Negro spirituals is made by a great black poet who wants to demonstrate to whites the originality of Negro music. Greenberg's article on American art is an episode in a battle he is fighting against a certain form of painting and aesthetic. All these people feel intimately bound up with what they are condemning or approving. It is themselves they are scourging or caressing. And don't think that any of them feels he is *doing* America *down* (with the exception, perhaps, of Wylie, though even then it is not certain). For a Frenchman, to expose an abuse is to do France down, because he sees the country in the past tense and as unchangeable. For an American, to do so is to pave the way for reform, as he sees his country in the future tense. When Greenberg writes that, in the US, art is left to 'the semi-educated, the gullible, the spinsters and the outmoded visionaries', you can be sure he regards this as a temporary state of affairs. These writers all take the view that America is as yet unfinished; they all write their articles from the standpoint of the future. It is these people we wanted to present, with their faith, their fury, their sense of passionate injustice, their lucidity too; with their goodwill, their way of judging and, at the same time, of *making* America. Each of these articles seems to me to be a face. A worried face, a face of stirring liberty. And it is precisely this we want to proffer to those readers who have not crossed the Atlantic and who do not yet know the strange, weary softness faces assume when the first lights are coming on on Broadway.

Les Temps modernes, August 1946.

Notes

1 When a gang of Rassemblement du peuple français supporters attempted to disrupt a political meeting in which I was taking part, a brawl ensued. An American who shared our ideas was amazed we did not call the police. I explained our reluctance, but he was still rather disconcerted: 'In our country,' he said, 'the police belong to all the citizens. We find it *natural* to call them in.'

2 Hence the misunderstanding in the Kravchenko case. Since rewriting is accepted practice, Kravchenko is regarded by Americans as the author of his book. We, by contrast, find it hard to see him as such.

3 Tennessee Valley Authority, created in 1933, by President Franklin D. Roosevelt as part of the New Deal.

4 Kisling and Masson have often complained that the cityscapes of the United States do not greatly encourage painting. This is partly, I believe, because the cities are already painted. They do not have the hesitant colours of ours. What can one do with these hues that are *already* art—or at least artifice—other than simply leave them where they are?

5 To give the reader an idea of this city, I suggest he tries to imagine not one town on the Côte d'Azur, but the entire Côte d'Azur from Cannes to Menton.

6 The rock labyrinth of Montpellier-le-Vieux near Mil-
lau (Aveyron, France) is a series of strange rock for-
mations that looks in places like a ruined town.
[Trans.]

7 This piece was written as an introduction to an issue
of *Les Temps modernes* on America. [Trans.]

8 To avoid anachronism, the term 'nègre' has been
translated as 'Negro' throughout. [Trans.]

PART THREE

materialism and revolution[1]

1. *the revolutionary myth*

Today's youth are uneasy. They no longer feel entitled
to be young and it is as though youth were not an age
of life but a class phenomenon, an unduly prolonged
childhood, an additional period of irresponsibility
granted to the children of the middle classes. The
workers pass without transition from adolescence to
manhood. And it seems that our times, which are
eliminating the European bourgeoisies, are also eliminating that abstract, metaphysical period which was
always said to be due 'its fling'. Out of shame at their
youth and that footloose quality that was once the
fashion, most of my ex-students have married young:
they have families while they are still studying. At the
end of each month they still receive a postal order

from their families, but it is not enough. They have to give lessons or translate or do supply teaching. They are half-workers, comparable in part to kept women and in part to homeworkers. They no longer take the time, as we did at their age, to play with ideas before adopting one. They are fathers and citizens; they vote; they have to commit themselves. This is doubtless no bad thing. After all, it is right they should be asked to choose from the outset whether they are for or against humanity, for or against the masses. But, if they take the former option, the difficulties begin, because they become persuaded that they have to slough off their subjectivity. If they contemplate doing this, however, being still inside their subjectivity, they do so for reasons that remain subjective. They consult *themselves* before plunging *themselves* into the water and, as a result, the more seriously they contemplate abandoning their subjectivity, the greater the importance it assumes. And they come to see, with some irritation, that their conception of objectivity is still a subjective one. And so they go round and round, unable to make a decision and, if they do make up their minds, they jump blindly for reasons of weariness or impatience.

Yet that is not an end to it. They are now being told to choose between materialism and idealism. They are told there is no middle way; it must be the one or the other. Yet, for most of them the principles of materialism seem philosophically false. They cannot understand how matter could give rise to the *idea* of matter. They protest, however, that they reject idealism with all their might and main; they know it is a myth that serves the propertied classes and that it is not a rigorous philosophy but quite a vague form of thinking, the function of which is to mask reality or absorb it into the idea. 'It makes no difference,' they are told. 'Since you are not materialists, you will be idealists in spite of yourselves and, though you resist the stale ruses of the academics, you will fall victim to a more subtle and even more dangerous illusion.'

So they are hounded even in their thoughts, which are poisoned at the roots, being condemned either to serve a philosophy they detest or, for reasons of discipline, adopt a doctrine in which they cannot believe. They have lost the carefree attitude proper to their age without acquiring the certainty of maturity. They are no longer footloose and yet they cannot commit themselves. They remain at the gates of Communism without daring to either enter or leave. They are not guilty: it is not their fault if the very people who invoke the dialectic want to force them to choose between two opposites and reject with the scornful name of Third Party the synthesis that would embrace the two. Since they are deeply sincere, since they wish to see a socialist regime, since they are ready to serve the Revolution with all their might, the only way to help them is to ask oneself, with them, whether materialism and the myth of objectivity are really demanded by the cause of the Revolution and whether there isn't a discrepancy between the revolutionary's actions and his ideology. For this reason, I turn now to materialism and attempt to examine it once again.

It seems that materialism's first move is to deny the existence of God and transcendent finality, its second to reduce the action of mind to that of matter, its third to eliminate subjectivity by reducing the world, with man in it, to a system of objects interconnected by universal relations. I conclude from this, in all good faith, that it is a metaphysical doctrine and that the materialists are metaphysicians. This is where they stop me right away: I am wrong, they say; there is nothing they hate so much as metaphysics. It is not even clear that philosophy is spared in their eyes. According to M. Naville, dialectical materialism is 'the expression of a progressive discovery of the world's interactions, a discovery that is in no way passive but involves the activity of the discoverer, the seeker and the struggler'. According to M. Garaudy, materialism's first move is to deny that there is any legitimate knowledge apart from scientific knowledge. And, for Mme Angrand, one cannot be a materialist unless one first rejects all a priori speculation.

These reproaches against metaphysics are old acquaintances: we met them in the last century in the writings of the positivists. But they, being more consistent, refused to pronounce on the existence of God because they regarded any conjectures one might form on that subject as unverifiable. And they had given up once and for all enquiring into the relations between mind and body, because they thought we could know nothing about it. It is clear, in fact, that M. Naville or Mme Angrand's atheism is not 'the expression of a progressive discovery'. It is a clear, a priori stance on a problem that infinitely exceeds our experience. Their position is also my own, but I did not see myself as any less of a metaphysician in denying existence to God than Leibniz was in granting it. And by what miracle would the materialist who criticizes the idealists for engaging in metaphysics when they reduce matter to spirit not be doing precisely the same thing when he reduces spirit to matter? Experience does not rule in favour of his doctrine any more than it does in favour of the opposing one. It confines itself to displaying the intimate connection between the physiological and the psychical, and that connection may be interpreted in a thousand different ways. When the materialist claims to be *certain* of his principles, his assurance can come only from a priori reasoning or intuition—in other words, from those very speculations he condemns. I understand now that materialism is a metaphysics hiding behind a positivism; but it is a self-destructive metaphysics, since, by undermining metaphysics on principle, it deprives its own assertions of any foundation.

By the same token, it destroys the positivism behind which it takes cover. It was out of modesty that

Comte's disciples reduced human knowledge to scientific learning alone: they confined reason within the narrow limits of our experience because it was only there that it showed itself to be effective. For them, the success of science was a fact, but it was a *human* fact. From the human standpoint, and for human beings, it is true that science succeeds. They were careful not to ask themselves whether the universe *in itself* supports and underwrites scientific rationalism, for the very good reason that they would have been obliged to step outside themselves and humanity to compare the universe as it *is* with the representation science provides of it and to assume the vantage point of God on man and the world. The materialist, for his part, is not so timid. He steps outside science, subjectivity and the human, and substitutes himself for the God he denies in order to contemplate the spectacle of the universe. He calmly writes, 'The materialistic outlook on nature means no more than simply conceiving nature just as it exists, without any foreign admixture.'[2]

What is happening, in this surprising text, is nothing short of the suppression of human subjectivity, that 'foreign admixture'. The materialist thinks that, by denying his subjectivity, he has made it vanish. But the trick performed here is an easy one to spot. *In order to* eliminate subjectivity, the materialist declares himself to be an *object*, that is to say, material for science. But once he has eliminated subjectivity in favour of the object, instead of seeing himself as a thing among other things, buffeted about by the undertow of the physical universe, he turns himself into an *objective observer* and claims to contemplate nature as it is, in the absolute. There is a play on the word 'objectivity' here; at times it means the passive quality of the object under observation and at others, the absolute value of an observer shorn of subjective weaknesses. So the materialist, having transcended all subjectivity and identified himself with pure objective truth, moves around in a world of objects inhabited by human objects. And when he returns from his travels, he reports what he has learnt: 'All that is rational is real,' he tells us, 'and all that is real is rational.'

Where does he get this rationalistic optimism? We can understand a Kantian making declarations about nature, since, in his view, reason constitutes experience. But the materialist does not accept that the world is the product of our constitutive activity. On the contrary, in his eyes it is we who are the product of the universe. Why, then, would we know that the real is rational, since we have not created it and reflect only a tiny part of it from day to day. At a pinch the success of science may lead us to think that this rationality is *probable*, but it may be a question of a local, statistical rationality. It may be valid for a certain order of magnitude and collapse above or below that limit.

Out of something which seems to us a reckless induction or, if you prefer, a postulate, materialism makes a certainty. For materialism there is no doubt. Reason is within man and outside him. And the leading journal of materialism calmly calls itself *La Pensée* [Thought], 'the organ of modern rationalism'. However, by a quite foreseeable dialectical reversal, materialist rationalism goes over into irrationalism and destroys itself: if the psychological fact is rigorously conditioned by the biological, and the biological fact is conditioned in turn by the physical state of the world, I can quite see how human consciousness may express the universe in the way an effect expresses its cause but not in the way a thought expresses its object. How could a reason that was captive, externally governed and manipulated by sequences of blind causes, still be *reason*? How could I believe in the principles of my deductions if it were merely external events that had deposited them in me and if, as Hegel says, 'reason is a bone'?[3] By what stroke of chance would the raw products of circumstance at the same time provide the keys to Nature? Moreover, look how Lenin speaks of our consciousness: 'It is merely the reflection of being—in the best of cases, an approximately exact reflection.' But who is to decide whether the present case—here, materialism—is the best of cases? We would have to be both outside and inside to make the comparison. And, as there can be no question of this, by the very terms of our declaration we have no criterion for the validity of the reflection, except internal, subjective criteria: its conformity with other reflections, its clarity, distinctness and permanence. In short, idealist criteria. And, even then, these will only determine a truth *for human beings*; and that truth, not being constructed like the truth proposed by the Kantians but received passively, will never be anything but a faith without foundation and a matter of habit.

Though dogmatic when it asserts that the universe produces thought, materialism goes over immediately into idealist scepticism. It lays down the inalienable rights of Reason with the one hand and takes them away with the other. It destroys positivism with a dogmatic rationalism, destroys both of these by the metaphysical assertion that man is a material object and destroys this assertion with the radical negation of all metaphysics. It pits science against metaphysics and, without realizing it, pits *a* metaphysics against science. Only ruins are left. How then could I be a materialist?

It will be objected that I have understood nothing, that I have confused the naïve materialism of Helvétius and d'Holbach with *dialectical* materialism. There is, I am told, a dialectical movement within nature whereby opposites, as they clash, are suddenly overcome and united in a new synthesis. And this new production goes over in turn into its opposite, to merge with it in another synthesis. I recognize at once the characteristic movement of the Hegelian dialectic here, a dialectic based entirely on the dynamism of Ideas. I recall how, in Hegel's philosophy, one idea leads to another, how each one produces its opposite. I know that the driving force behind this immense movement is the attraction exerted by the future on the present and by the whole, even when it does not exist yet, on its parts. This is as true of partial syntheses as it is of the absolute Totality, which ultimately will be Mind or Spirit [*Geist*]. The principle of this Dialectic is, then, that a whole governs its parts; that an idea tends of itself to complete and enrich itself; that the progress of consciousness is not linear, like that of cause and effect, but synthetic and multi-dimensional, since each idea retains within itself and assimilates to itself the totality of previous ideas; that the structure of the concept is not the mere juxtaposition of invariable elements which could, if need be, join with other elements to produce new combinations, but an organization whose unity is such that its secondary structures could not be considered in isolation from the whole without becoming 'abstract' and losing their nature.

One readily accepts this dialectic in the realm of ideas: ideas are naturally synthetic. Only, we are told, Hegel had stood it on its head and it is, in reality, specific to matter. And if you ask what matter we are speaking of, you are told that there is only one—the matter of which scientists speak. Now, matter is characterized by its inertia. That means it is incapable of producing anything by itself. It is a vehicle for movement and energy, but that movement and energy always come to it from outside: it borrows them and yields them up again. The mainspring of all dialectics is the idea of totality. In dialectics, phenomena are never isolated occurrences; when they occur together, they do so always within the higher unity of a whole and they are connected by internal relations, that is to say, the presence of one modifies the other in its deep nature. But the world of science is quantitative. And quantity is precisely the opposite of dialectical unity. Only in appearance is a sum a unity. The elements that make it up have, in fact, only relations of continuity and simultaneity between them. They are present together, and that is all. A numerical unit is in no sense influenced by the co-presence of another unit; it remains inert and separate within the number it helps to form. And things have to be this way if we are to be able to count. For if two phenomena occurred in intimate union and modified each other reciprocally, it would be impossible to decide whether we were dealing with two separate terms or with one. Thus, as scientific matter represents, so to speak, the realization of quantity, science is, in its inmost concerns, its principles and its methods, the opposite of dialectics.

When science speaks of forces that are applied at a material point, its first concern is to assert their independence: each acts as though it were alone. If it studies the attraction bodies exert on one another, it is careful to define that attraction as a strictly external relation or, in other words, to reduce it to changes in the direction and velocity of their movements. Science occasionally uses the word 'synthesis', for example in relation to chemical combinations. But it never does so in the Hegelian sense. The particles that come into combination retain their properties; if an atom of oxygen combines with atoms of sulphur and hydrogen to form sulphuric acid or with hydrogen alone to form water, it remains identical to itself. Neither the water nor the acid are genuine totalities that change and govern their components. They are mere passive resultants or *states*. The entire effort of biology is aimed at reducing alleged living syntheses to physico-chemical processes. And when M. Naville, who is a materialist, feels the need to create a materialist psychology, he turns to 'behaviourism', which regards human conduct as a sum of conditioned reflexes. Nowhere in the world of science do we meet any organic totalities. The scientist's tool is analysis; his aim is everywhere to reduce the complex to the simple and the recomposition he subsequently effects is simply a counter-check, whereas the dialectician, on principle, regards complexes as irreducible.

Admittedly, Engels does claim that, 'nature is the test of dialectics, and it must be said for modern natural science that it has furnished . . . materials for this test, and has thus proved that in the last analysis nature's process is dialectical and not metaphysical, that it does not move in an eternal uniform and constantly repeated circle, but passes through a real history.'[4] And he cites the example of Darwin to support his argument: ' (Darwin) dealt a severe blow to the metaphysical conception of nature by proving that the organic world of today . . . is all a product of a process of development that has been in progress for millions of years.'[5] But first it is clear that the notion of *natural history* is absurd. History is characterized neither by change nor by the pure and simple action of the past; it is defined by the intentional re-appropriation of the past by the present: there can only be a human history. Besides, if Darwin has shown that species derive from one another, his attempt to explain this is of a mechanical, not a dialectical, order. He accounts for individual differences by the theory of small variations. And each of these variations is, in his view, not in fact the effect of a 'process of development' but of mechanical chance. Statistically, it is impossible in a group of individuals of a same species for there not to be some that are greater in size, weight, strength or some particular detail. As for the struggle for existence, it cannot *produce* a new synthesis by merging opposites; it has strictly negative effects, since it *eliminates* the weakest once and for all. To grasp this, we need only compare the outcome with the truly dialectical ideal of the class struggle. In the latter case, the proletariat will merge the bourgeois class into itself in the unity of a classless society. In the struggle for existence, the strong purely and simply wipe out the weak. Lastly, the chance advantage does not *develop*: it remains inert and is passed on unchanged by heredity. It is a *state* and that state will not modify itself by an inner dynamism to produce a higher degree of organization. Another chance variation will simply be added to it from outside and the process of elimination will be reproduced mechanically. Should we conclude from this that Engels is being frivolous or dishonest? In order to prove that nature has a history, he employs a scientific hypothesis explicitly intended to reduce all natural history to mechanical sequences.

Is Engels more serious when he speaks of physics?

'In physics . . . every change is a passing of quantity into quality, as a result of quantitative change of some form of movement either inherent in a body or imparted to it. "For example, the temperature of water has at first no effect on its liquid state; but as the temperature of liquid water rises or falls, a moment arrives when this state of cohesion changes and the water is converted in one case into steam and in the other into ice." '[6]

But he is confusing us here with smoke and mirrors. Scientific research is not at all concerned, in fact, with demonstrating the transition from quantity to quality.

It starts out from the perceptible quality, conceived as an illusory, subjective appearance, in order to discover the quantity behind it that is conceived as the truth of the universe. Engels naïvely regards quantity as though it presented itself *initially* as a pure quantity. But, in fact, it first appears as a quality: it is that state of unease or contentment that makes us button up our raincoat or, conversely, take it off. The scientist reduced this perceptible quality to a quantity when he agreed to substitute for the vague message from our senses the measurement of the cubic expansion of a liquid. The transformation of water into steam is an equally quantitative phenomenon for him. Or, to put it another way, it exists for him only *as* quantity. It is by pressure that he will define steam—or by a kinetic theory that will reduce it to a certain quantitative state (position or velocity) of its molecules. We must, then, choose. Either we remain on the ground of the perceptible quality and steam is then a quality, as also is temperature; we are not doing science, but are observing the action of one quality on another. Or we view temperature as a quantity, but then the transition from the liquid to the gaseous state will be defined scientifically as a quantitative change—that is to say, by a measurable pressure exerted on a piston or by measurable relations between molecules. For the scientist, quantity produces quantity; the law is a quantitative formula and science has no symbol at its disposal to express quality as such. What Engels claims to present to us as a scientific approach is the pure and simple movement of his mind which goes from the scientific universe to that of naïve realism and then returns to the scientific world to recover the world of pure sensation. And even if we conceded all this to him, does this toing-and-froing of thought in the least resemble a dialectical process? Where does he see a progression? Let us accept that the change of temperature, regarded as quantitative, produces a qualitative transformation of water: water is changed into steam. What then? It will exert pressure on an escape valve and open it; it will rise into the air, cool and become water again. Where is the progression? I see a cycle. Of course, water is no longer contained in the recipient but is outside on the grass and earth in the form of dew. But by what metaphysics can one see this change of place as an advance?[7]

It will perhaps be objected that some modern theories, such as Einstein's, are synthetic. In his system, as we know, there are no longer any isolated elements: every reality is defined in relation to the universe. There is much that could be said about this but I shall confine myself to observing that what we have here is not a synthesis at all, since the relations that can be established between the various structures of a synthesis are *internal* and *qualitative* whereas the relations that enable us to define a position or a mass in Einstein's theories remain *quantitative* and *external*. Moreover, this is not the key point. Whether we are speaking of Newton, Archimedes, Laplace or Einstein, the scientist does not study the concrete totality but the general and abstract conditions of the universe. Not *this* event, which takes light, heat and life and melds them into something particular, known as 'the glistening of the sun through foliage on a summer's day', but light *in general*, calorific phenomena, the *general* conditions of life. It is not a question of examining *this* refraction through *this* piece of glass which has its history and which, from a certain standpoint, can be seen as the concrete synthesis of the universe, but the conditions of possibility of refraction *in gen-*

eral. Science is made up of *concepts* in the Hegelian sense of the term. Dialectics, on the other hand, is essentially the play of *notions*. We know that, in Hegel's conception, the notion organizes and fuses together concepts in the organic, living unity of concrete reality. The Earth, the Renaissance, Colonization in the nineteenth century and Nazism are understood as *notions*; Being, Light and Energy are abstract concepts. Dialectical enrichment lies in the passage from abstract to concrete, that is to say, from elementary concepts to ever more complex notions. Thus, the movement of the dialectic is the reverse of the movement of science.

'It's true,' a Communist intellectual admitted to me, 'that science and dialectics pull in opposite directions. But this is because science expresses the bourgeois viewpoint, which is analytical. Our dialectic, by contrast, is the very thinking of the proletariat.' I can accept this, though Soviet science doesn't seem to differ very much in its methods from the science of the bourgeois states. But if this is the case, why do the Communists borrow arguments and evidence from science on which to base their materialism? The basic spirit of science is, I believe, materialistic. But here we are told that it is analytic and bourgeois. The positions are, as a result, reversed and I can clearly see two classes in struggle: the one, the bourgeoisie, is materialist, its method of thinking is analytic, its ideology is science; the other, the proletariat, is idealist, its method of thinking is synthesis, its ideology is dialectics. And since there is struggle between the classes, there must be incompatibility between the ideologies. But not at all: we are told that dialectics is the crowning glory of science and makes use of its results; we are told that the bourgeoisie, drawing on analysis and, consequently, reducing the higher to the lower, is idealist, whereas the proletariat—which thinks in terms of synthesis and is led by the revolutionary ideal—even though it asserts the irreducibility of a synthesis to its elements, is materialist. Who can make any sense of all this?

Let us come back, then, to science which, whether it is bourgeois or not, has at least proved itself. We know what it teaches about matter. A material object, which is animated from without, conditioned by the total state of the world, subject to forces that always have their origin elsewhere, and made up of elements that combine without interpenetrating and remain alien to it, is external to itself; its most evident properties are statistical; they are merely the resultant of the motion of the molecules that make it up. Nature, as Hegel so profoundly says, is externality. How are we to find a place in this externality for that movement of absolute internalization that is dialectics? Is it not clear from the very idea of synthesis that life is irreducible to matter and human consciousness irreducible to life? Between modern science, object of materialist faith and love, and the dialectics the materialists claim as their instrument and method, there is the same discrepancy as we noted above between their positivism and their metaphysics: the one wrecks the other. And so they will tell you at one point that life is merely a complex sequence of physico-chemical phenomena and at another, with the same imperturbability, that it is an irreducible moment of the natural dialectic. Or, rather, they attempt, dishonestly to think both at the same time. One has the sense, from their confused discourse, that they have invented the slippery, contradictory notion of reducible irreducibilities.

M. Garaudy is satisfied with this. But when you hear him speak you are struck by his wavering: at times he asserts, in the abstract, that mechanistic determinism has had its day and that it must be replaced by dialectics; at others, when he attempts to explain a concrete situation, he comes back to causal relations, which are linear and presuppose the absolute externality of the cause to the effect. It is perhaps this notion of *cause* that best shows up the great intellectual confusion into which the materialists have fallen. When I challenged M. Naville to define, within the framework of the dialectic, this famous causality he is so fond of employing, he seemed disconcerted and had no reply. How well I understand him! I would be inclined to say that the notion of cause remains hanging between scientific relations and dialectical syntheses. Materialism being, as we have seen, an *explanatory* metaphysics (it attempts to *explain* some social phenomena by others, the psychological sphere by the biological, the biological by physico-chemical laws), it uses the causal schema on principle. But, since it sees science as the explanation of the universe, it turns to science and is surprised to find that the causal connection is not scientific. Where is the cause in Joule's Law or Mariotte's, in Archimedes' Principle or Carnot's? Science most often establishes functional relations between phenomena and chooses the independent variable that suits its purpose. It is, moreover, strictly impossible to express the qualitative relation of causality in mathematical language. Most physical laws simply take the form of functions of the type $y = f(x)$. Others establish numerical constants. Yet others give us phases of irreversible phenomena, but without our being able to say that one of these phases is the *cause* of the next (can we say that in karyokinesis, nuclear dissolution is the *cause* of the segmentation of the protoplasmic filament?). So materialist causality remains up in the air. The fact is that it has its origin in the metaphysical attempt to reduce mind to matter and explain the psychological by the physical. Disappointed that there is *too little* in science to bolster his causal explanations, the materialist reverts, then, to the dialectic. But there is *too much* in the dialectic. The causal link is linear and the cause remains external to its effect. Moreover, there is never more in the effect than in the cause: otherwise, from the standpoint of causal explanation, that residue would remain unexplained. Dialectical progress, by contrast, is a totalizing progress: at each new stage it looks back on the set of positions

171

transcended and embraces them all. And the move from one stage to another is always an enrichment: there is always *more* in the synthesis than in the thesis and antithesis combined. So the materialists' cause can neither be backed by science nor hang itself on the dialectic: it remains a vulgar, practical notion, the mark of materialism's unceasing effort to bend the one towards the other and unite two mutually exclusive methods by force; it is the very type of the false synthesis and the use made of it is a dishonest one.

Nowhere is this more evident than in the Marxists' attempts to study 'superstructures'. For Marxists, these are, in a sense, 'reflections' of the mode of production.

> Hence, if in different periods of the history of society different social ideas, theories, views and political institutions are to be observed; if under the slave system we encounter certain social ideas, theories, views and political institutions, under feudalism others, and under capitalism others still, this is not to be explained by the 'nature', the 'properties' of the ideas, theories, views and political institutions themselves but by the

different conditions of the material life of
society at different periods of social development. Whatever is the being of a society,
whatever are the conditions of material life
of a society, such are the ideas, theories, political views and political institutions of that
society.[8]

The use of the term 'reflection' and that of the
verb 'determine', together with the general tone of
the passage, tell us all we need to know: we are on the
terrain of determinism; the superstructure is entirely
supported and conditioned by the social situation it
reflects; the relation of the mode of production to
the political institution is one of cause to effect. It was
on this basis that a naïve thinker once saw Spinoza's
philosophy as an exact reflection of the Dutch grain
trade. But at the same time, because Marxist propaganda needs it to be this way, ideologies must, to a degree, have a certain self-sufficiency and be able to act
back on the social situation that conditions them. This
means, in short, that they must have a certain autonomy from the substructures. For this reason, Marxists
have recourse here to the dialectic and present the superstructure as a synthesis which, though it emanates

from the conditions of production and material life, has a nature and laws of development that are genuinely 'independent'. In the same pamphlet, Stalin writes:

> New social ideas and theories arise only after the development of the material life of society has set new tasks before society . . . New social ideas and theories arise precisely because they are necessary to society, because it is *impossible* to carry out the urgent tasks of development of the material life of society without their organizing, mobilizing and transforming action.[9]

In this text, necessity has, as we see, assumed a quite different aspect: an idea arises because it is necessary for the accomplishment of a new task. In other words, the task, before even being accomplished, *calls forth* the idea that will 'facilitate' its accomplishment. The idea is postulated and arises out of a vacuum which it then fills. The word 'arise' is actually the one Stalin uses a few lines later. This action of the future, this necessity which is coterminous with purpose, this organizing, mobilizing and transforming power of the idea clearly brings us back to the terrain of the

Hegelian dialectic. But how can I believe in both of Stalin's assertions at once? Is the idea 'determined by the social situation' or 'arising out of the new tasks to be accomplished'? Should we believe with him that 'the spiritual life of society is a reflection of [this] objective reality, a *reflection* of being'—that is to say, a derived, borrowed reality, that has no *being* of its own but is more or less analogous to the Stoics' 'lecta'? Or should I, rather, declare with Lenin that 'ideas become living realities when they live in the consciousness of the masses'? On the one hand, a causal and linear relation, implying the inertia of the effect or reflection and on the other a dialectical, synthetic relation which would imply that the final synthesis turns back to the partial syntheses that have produced it to embrace them and merge them into itself; therefore, that mental life, though emanating from the material life of society, turns back to it and absorbs it whole. The materialists do not decide: they waver between the two. They affirm dialectical progression in the abstract, but their concrete studies are mostly limited to timeworn explanations along the lines of Hippolyte Taine in terms of 'milieu' and 'moment'.[10]

There is more—beginning with the question, what precisely is this concept of *matter* the dialecticians use? If they borrow it from science, then it will be the poorest concept that will merge into other concepts to arrive at a concrete notion, the richest one. This notion will, in the end, include the concept of matter within it as one of its structures; but it will not be that concept that explains the notion but, rather, the notion that explains the concept. In this case, it is acceptable to start out from matter as the emptiest of abstractions. It is acceptable also to start out from being, as Hegel does. The difference is not great, though the Hegelian starting-point, being the more abstract, is the better choice. But if we really have to *invert* the Hegelian dialectic and 'set it back on its feet', we must admit that matter, chosen as the starting point of the dialectical movement, does not appear to Marxists as the poorest concept but the richest notion. It is identified with the entire universe; it is the unity of all phenomena. Thoughts, life and individuals are merely modes of matter; it is, in short, the great Spinozist totality. Yet, if this is the case, and if Marxist matter is the exact counterpart of Hegelian spirit, we arrive at the paradoxical outcome that Marxism, in order to set the dialectic back on its feet, has put the richest notion at the beginning. And doubtless, for Hegel, Spirit comes at the beginning, but it does so as virtuality, as summons: the dialectic is merely identical with its history. For Marxists, by contrast, it is the whole of matter in action that is given at the outset, and the dialectic, whether it applies to the history of species or to the evolution of human societies, is only ever the re-tracing of the partial becoming of one of the modes of that reality. But if the dialectic is not, then, the very generation of the world, if it is not progressive enrichment, it is nothing. In obligingly taking up dialectics once again, Marxism has dealt it a death blow. It has unthinkingly killed it with kindness. How, you will ask, has this gone unnoticed? It is because our materialists have built up a slippery, contradictory concept of 'matter'. At times it is the poorest abstraction and at others, the richest concrete totality; as the need dictates. They jump from the one to the other and conceal the one behind the other. And when, finally, you run them to ground and they have no escape, they declare that materialism is a method, an orientation of mind; if you pushed them a little, they would say it was a style of life. They would not be so wrong in this and, for my part, I would be happy to regard it as one of the forms of the *esprit de sérieux* and the flight from oneself.[11] If materialism is a *human attitude*, with all that that entails in terms of subjectivity, contradictoriness and sentimentality, then it should not be presented to us as a rigorous philosophy, as the doctrine of objectivity.

I have seen conversions to materialism. It is something taken up as others might take up religion. I would happily define it as the subjectivity of those ashamed of their subjectivity. It is also, of course, the ill-humour of those who suffer in their bodies and know the reality of hunger, illness, manual labour and everything that can sap a human being's vigour. In a word, it is a doctrine of first resort. Now, the first resort is perfectly legitimate, especially when it expresses the spontaneous reaction of oppressed people to their situation—but that does not make it the right one. It always contains a truth, but it goes beyond that truth. To assert, against idealism, the crushing reality of the material world, is not necessarily to be a materialist. We shall come back to this point.

But how does it come about that, in falling from heaven to earth, dialectics retained its necessity? Hegelian consciousness has no need to *advance the dialectical hypothesis*. It is not a pure objective witness watching the generation of ideas from outside. It is itself dialectical; it engenders itself by the laws of synthetic progression. There is no need at all for it to *presuppose* necessity in connections; it *is* that necessity, it lives it. And its certainty does not come to it from some evidence more or less open to criticism, but from the progressive identification of the dialectic of consciousness with the consciousness of the dialectic. If, on the other hand, the dialectic represents the mode of development of the material world, if consciousness, rather than being wholly identified with the entire dialectic, is merely a 'reflection of being', a partial product, a moment of synthetic progress, if, instead of watching its own generation from within, it is invaded from outside by feelings and ideologies that have their roots elsewhere, which it suffers passively without producing them, then it is merely a link in a chain whose beginning and end are very far apart.

And what can it say about the chain that is *certain* unless it is itself the whole of the chain? The dialectic deposits a few effects in it and carries on its way; considering these effects, thought may judge that they attest to the probable existence of a synthetic mode of progression. Or, alternatively, it may form conjectures on the consideration of external phenomena: in any event, it will have to content itself with regarding the dialectic as a working hypothesis, as a method that must be tried and of which success will be the test. How does it come about that materialists regard this research method as a structure of the universe; how does it come about that they avow themselves certain that the 'interconnection and interdependence of phenomena as established by the dialectical method, are a law of the development of moving matter',[12] since the sciences of nature proceed in a spirit contrary to this and use strictly opposite methods, and since historical science is only at its first tentative beginnings? It is clearly the case that, in transporting the dialectic from one world to the other, they did not wish to forego the advantages it had in the first world. They retained the dialectic's necessity and certainty, while actually giving up such means as they had of verifying them. They wished to give matter the mode of synthetic development that belongs to the idea alone, and they borrowed from the idea's reflection in itself a type of certainty that has no place in the experience of the world. But, as a result, matter itself becomes idea: it nominally retains its opacity, inertia and externality, but it offers also a perfect translucency, since its internal processes can be decided on principle and with total certainty; it is a synthesis, it progresses by constant enrichment.

Let us be clear about this; there is no simultaneous transcendence of materialism and idealism here.[13] Opacity and transparency, externality and interiority, inertia and synthetic progression are merely juxtaposed in the spurious unity of 'dialectical materialism'. Matter has remained the matter that science reveals to us. There has been no combination of opposites, for want of a new concept that would really merge them into itself and that would be neither precisely matter nor idea. It is not by surreptitiously attributing the qualities of the one to the other that their opposition can be surmounted. It must, in fact, be admitted

181

that, in claiming to be dialectical, materialism 'goes over into' idealism. Just as Marxists claim to be positivists and wreck their positivism by the use they implicitly make of metaphysics, just as they proclaim their rationalism and wreck it by their conception of the origin of thought, so they deny their principle—materialism—in the very moment that they posit it, by a furtive recourse to idealism.[14]

This confusion is reflected in the materialist's subjective attitude to his own doctrine. 'Materialism *holds that* . . . ,' says Stalin. But why does it hold this? Why hold that God does not exist, that mind is a reflection of matter, that the development of the world is a product of contrary forces, that there is an objective truth, that there are no unknowables in the world but only things as yet unknown? We are not told. Only, if it is true that, 'arising out of the new tasks set by the development of the material life of society, new social ideas and theories force their way through, become the possession of the masses, mobilize and organize them against the moribund forces of society, and thus facilitate the overthrow of these forces, which hamper the development of the material life of society',[15] then it seems clear that these ideas are adopted by the proletariat because they account for its present situation and needs, because they are the most effective instrument in its struggle against the bourgeois class. 'The fall of the utopians, including the Narodniks, anarchists and Socialist-Revolutionaries, was due, among other things,' writes Stalin in this same work,

> to the fact that they did not recognize the primary role which the conditions of the material life of society play in the development of society, and, sinking to idealism, did not base their practical activities on the needs of the development of the material life of society, but, independently of and in spite of these needs, on 'ideal plans' and 'all-embracing projects', divorced from the real life of society. The strength and vitality of Marxism–Leninism lies in the fact that it does base its practical activity on the needs of the development of the material life of society and never divorces itself from the real life of society.[16]

Though materialism may be the best instrument for action, its truth is pragmatic in nature: it is true for the working class because it works for them. And, since social progress must be made by the working class, it is truer than idealism, which for a time served the interests of the bourgeoisie when it was the rising class and cannot but hamper the development of the material life of society today. But when the proletariat has finally absorbed the bourgeois class into itself and brought about the classless society, new tasks will appear from which new ideas and social theories will 'arise': materialism will have had its day, since it is the thought of the working class and there will no longer be a working class. Grasped objectively and as the expression of the needs and tasks of a class, materialism becomes an *opinion*. In other words, it is a force of mobilization, transformation and organization, the objective reality of which can be gauged by its power of action. And this opinion that passes itself off as a certitude carries within it its own destruction since, on the basis of its own principles, it must regard itself as objective fact, as reflection of being and as object of science, yet at the same time it destroys the science that must analyse and establish it—at least as opinion. The reasoning is clearly circular and the whole system remains up in the air, perpetually hovering between being and nothingness.

The Stalinist gets out of all this by faith. If he 'holds that' materialism is true, it is because he wants to act and change the world. When you are engaged in such a vast undertaking, you don't have time to quibble over the choice of principles justifying it. He believes in Marx, Lenin and Stalin; he accepts the principle of authority and, lastly, he retains the blind, calm faith that materialism is a certainty. This conviction will colour his general attitude to all the ideas proposed to him. Examine one of his doctrines or concrete assertions at all closely and he will tell you he has no time to lose, that the situation is urgent, that he must first act, deal with the most pressing matters and work for the Revolution. There will be time later on to question principles—or, rather, they will question themselves. For the moment, however, all challenges to his thinking have to be rejected, as they have a weakening effect. This is all very well, but when, in his turn, he attacks or criticizes bourgeois thought or some intellectual position he regards as reactionary, then he claims to hold the truth. The same principles, which a few moments ago he told you it was not quite the time to dispute, suddenly become solid facts. They shift from the level of useful opinions to truths. 'The

JEAN-PAUL SARTRE

Trotskyites,' you say to him, 'are wrong; but they aren't police informers, as you claim. You know perfectly well that they aren't.' 'On the contrary,' he will reply, 'I absolutely know that they are. Ultimately what they think is a matter of indifference. Subjectivity doesn't exist. But *objectively* they are playing the bourgeoisie's game; they're *behaving* like provocateurs and informers, since unconsciously playing into the hands of the police and deliberately collaborating with them amount to the same thing.' You reply that this is precisely the point: they are not the same thing and, in all *objectivity*, the behaviour of the Trotskyite and the police officer are not alike. He retorts that the one is as harmful as the other and the effect of both is to retard the advance of the working class. And if you keep at him, if you show him there are many ways of slowing that advance and they are not all equivalent even in their effects, he replies haughtily that these distinctions, even if true, do not interest him. We are in a period of struggle. The situation is simple and the positions clear-cut. Why complicate matters? The Communist militant shouldn't bother his head about these nuances. And we are back once more with pragmatism,

186

so that the proposition 'the Trotskyite is an informer' wavers perpetually between the status of useful opinion and objective truth.[17]

Nothing demonstrates the ambiguity of the Marxist notion of truth better than the ambivalence in the Communist attitude to scientists. The Communists appeal to scientists, exploit their discoveries and present their thinking as the only type of valid knowledge. Yet they never lower their guard towards them. Insofar as they base themselves on the rigorous notion of *objectivity*, they need the scientists' critical spirit, their taste for research and for attacking established opinion, their clearsightedness, which rejects authority and reverts always to experiment or rational proof. But they are distrustful of these same virtues inasmuch as they are believers and inasmuch as science calls all beliefs into question. If the scientist brings his scientific qualities to the party, if he claims the right to examine principles, he becomes an 'intellectual' and his dangerous freedom of thought, an expression of his relative material independence, finds itself opposed by the faith of the militant worker who, by his very situation, *needs* to believe in the directives of his leaders.[18]

This, then, is the materialism for which they want me to opt: a monster, an elusive Proteus, a great vague, contradictory sham. They ask me to choose, this very day, in all freedom and all lucidity, and what I must choose freely and lucidly, with the best of my thought, is a doctrine that destroys thought. I know there is no other salvation for humanity than the liberation of the working class: I know this *before* being a materialist and on the simple inspection of the facts. I know the interests of the mind lie with the proletariat: is that any reason for me to demand of my thought, which brought me to this point, that it destroy itself? Is it any reason to force it now to relinquish its criteria, to embrace self-contradiction, to be torn between incompatible arguments, to lose even the clear consciousness of itself, to launch forth blindly on a giddy race towards faith? 'Get down on your knees and you will believe,' says Pascal. What the materialist does is very similar to this.

Now, if it were just a matter of me getting down on my knees and if, by that sacrifice, I could ensure humanity's happiness, I would no doubt consent to do so. But it is actually a question of giving up everyone's entitlement to free criticism, to facts and, in a word, to truth. I am told we shall get these things back later. But there is no proof this is the case. How could I believe in a promise made in the name of self-destroying principles? I know only one thing: my mind has, this very day, to throw in the towel. Have I fallen into this unacceptable dilemma: to betray the proletariat in order to serve truth or to betray truth in the name of the proletariat?

If I consider the materialist faith not in terms of its content but of its history, as a social phenomenon, I can clearly see it is not a whim of intellectuals nor a mere error on the part of a philosopher. As far back as I go, I find it associated with the revolutionary attitude. Epicurus, the first man actually to try to free men from their fears and their chains, the first man to try to abolish slavery on his land, was a materialist. The materialism of the great philosophers—and, indeed, that of the '*sociétés de pensée*'—played no small part in paving the way for the French Revolution. And, lastly, using an argument very closely akin to that used by Catholics in defending their faith, the Communists are fond of arguing that, 'if materialism were wrong, how do you explain how it has united the working class, enabled them to be led into battle, and brought us, despite the most violent repression, this succession of victories in the last half century?' This argument, which is a scholastic one, of proof a posteriori by success, is not insignificant.

It has to be said that materialism is today the philosophy of the proletariat, precisely insofar as the proletariat is revolutionary. This austere, mendacious doctrine is the bearer of the purest, most ardent hopes; this theory which denies human freedom root and branch has become the instrument of humanity's most thoroughgoing liberation. This indicates that its content is suited to 'mobilizing and organizing' revolutionary forces; and that there is a deep connection between the *situation* of an oppressed class and the materialist *expression* of that situation. But we cannot conclude from this that materialism is a philosophy or, still less, that it *is* the truth.

Insofar as it enables coherent action to be mounted, insofar as it expresses a concrete situation, insofar as millions of people find hope and an image of their condition in it, materialism must undoubtedly contain some truth. But this in no sense means that it is wholly true as a doctrine. The truths it contains may be shrouded and drowned in error; it may be that, in order to cope with the urgent tasks before it, revolutionary thinking has thrown up a rapid, temporary construction for getting to those truths, has developed what dressmakers call a basted garment. In that case, there is much more in materialism than the revolutionary requires. There is also much less, for this hasty, forced tacking-together of truths prevents them from acquiring a spontaneous structure among themselves and attaining their true unity. Materialism is indisputably the *only myth* that fits with revolutionary exigencies, and the politician looks no further. The myth serves him, he adopts it. But if his undertaking is to stand the test of time, it is not a myth he needs but the *Truth*. It is the philosopher's business to make the truths contained in materialism hold together and, little by little, to constitute a philosophy that suits revolutionary exigencies as exactly as the myth does. And the best means for identifying these truths within the error in which they are immersed is to determine those exigencies from an attentive examination of the revolutionary attitude; to retrace, in each case, the path by which they have given rise to the call for a materialist representation of the universe; and to see whether they have not, each time, been deflected and diverted from their initial meaning. Perhaps if they are freed from the myth that both crushes them and conceals them from themselves, they will yield the broad lineaments of a coherent philosophy that has the advantage over materialism of being a *true* description of nature and human relations.

ii. *the philosophy of revolution*

The Nazis and their collaborators proceeded by blurring ideas. The Pétain regime called itself a Revolution, and things reached such a point of absurdity that one day *La Gerbe* ran the following headline: 'Conserve!—this is the motto of the National Revolution'. It is right, then, that we recall here a number of elementary truths. To avoid any presuppositions, we shall adopt the a posteriori definition given by historian Albert Mathiez: in his view, a revolution occurs when a change in institutions is accompanied by a profound modification of the regime of ownership.

We shall term that party or person within a party revolutionary whose acts intentionally work towards

193

such a revolution. And the first thing we have to say is that not everyone can become a revolutionary. Doubtless, the existence of a strong, organized party with revolutionary aims may exert its attraction on individuals or groups of all origins, but the organization of that party can be the work only of persons of a determinate social condition. In other words, revolutionaries are *in situation*. They are clearly to be found only among the oppressed, but being oppressed is not enough to make one desire to be a revolutionary. We may class the Jews among the oppressed—and the same holds true in some countries for ethnic minorities—but many of them are oppressed within the bourgeoisie and, as they share the privileges of the class that oppresses them, they cannot without contradiction work towards the destruction of those privileges. In the same way, we cannot term the feudal nationalists of the colonies revolutionary, nor the American blacks, even though their interests may coincide with those of the party working towards revolution: the integration of these groups into society is not complete. What the former call for is the *return* to an earlier state of affairs: they wish to *recover* their supremacy and break the ties that bind them to the colonial society. What American blacks and bourgeois Jews want is equal rights, which in no way implies a structural change in the regime of property rights. They merely wish to share in the privileges of their oppressors, which is to say that they are, ultimately, seeking a more complete integration.

Revolutionaries are in a situation where they cannot in any sense share in these privileges. It is by the destruction of the class oppressing them that they can obtain their demands. This means that their oppression is not, like that of the Jews or the American Negroes, a secondary and, as it were, lateral characteristic of the social regime in question but that it is, in fact, constitutive. Revolutionaries are, therefore, both oppressed persons and the keystone of the society oppressing them. To put it more plainly, it is as an oppressed person that the revolutionary is indispensable to that society. That is to say, the revolutionary is one of those who *work* for the dominant class.

Revolutionaries are necessarily oppressed persons and workers, and it is as workers that they are oppressed. This dual character of producer and oppressed individual suffices to define the situation of revolutionaries, but not the revolutionaries themselves. The *canuts* of Lyon or the workers of the 1848 'June days' were not revolutionaries, but rioters. They were fighting for a particular improvement of their lot, not for its radical transformation. This means their situation was confined to themselves alone and, taken overall, they accepted it: they accepted being wage workers and working on machines they did not own; they acknowledged the rights of the owners and obeyed the morality of that class. It was simply the case that, within a set of circumstances they had neither transcended nor even recognized, they were calling for an increase in wages.

Revolutionaries, by contrast, are defined by the *transcendence* of the situation in which they find themselves. And because they go beyond that situation in the direction of a radically new one, they can grasp it as a synthetic whole or, to put it another way, they make it exist for them as a totality. It is on the basis of this transcendence towards the future, then, and from the standpoint of the future, that they *realize* that situation. Instead of appearing to them, as it does to the resigned victims of oppression, as a definitive, a priori structure, it is for them only one moment of the universe. Since they wish to change it, since they view it at the very outset from the standpoint of history, they regard themselves as historical agents.

From the very beginning, then, by this self-projection into the future, they escape the society that is crushing them and gain a vantage point that enables them to understand it: they see a human history at one with human destiny, a history in which the change they wish to effect is, if not the goal, then at least an essential step on the way. History appears to them as progress, since they consider the state they wish to lead us to as better than the one in which we currently find ourselves. At the same time they see human relations from the viewpoint of work, since work is their lot. Now, work is, among other things, a direct connection between human beings and the universe: it is humanity's purchase on nature and, at the same time, a primordial type of relationship between human beings. It is, therefore, an essential attitude of human reality which, in the unity of a single project, both 'exists' and makes exist, in their mutual dependence, its relation to nature and its relation to others. And, insofar as they call for their liberation *as workers*, they know very well that this cannot come about by their mere integration into the privileged class. Rather, what they wish is for the relations of solidarity they maintain with other workers to become the very model of human relations. They wish, therefore, for the liberation of the oppressed class in its entirety. Unlike the rebel, who stands alone, the revolutionaries' self-understanding requires relations of solidarity with their class.

Thus, because they are aware of the social structure on which they depend, revolutionaries demand a philosophy that takes account of their situation and, since their action has no meaning unless it involves the fate of all humanity, that philosophy has to be total: that is to say, it has to provide a total elucidation of the human condition. And since they are themselves, as workers, an essential structure of society and the hinge between human beings and nature, they can have no truck with a philosophy that would not primarily and centrally express the original relationship of man to the world, which is, precisely, the coordinated action of the one on the other. Lastly, since this philosophy arises out of a historical enterprise and has to represent for the person requiring it a certain mode of historicization which that person has chosen, it necessarily has to present the course of history as oriented or, at least, as capable of orientation. And since it arises out of action and focuses back on action, which requires it for its elucidation, it is not a contemplation of the world but must itself be an action. Let us be clear that it is not something super-added to the revolutionary effort; it is indistinguishable from that effort. It is contained in the original project of the worker who joins the party of revolution, since any project to change the world is inseparable from a certain understanding which discloses the world from the standpoint of the change in it that one is trying to bring about. The revolutionary philosopher's task will consist, then, in identifying and making explicit the great guiding themes of the revolutionary attitude, and that philosophical task is itself an act, since the philosopher can identify those themes only if he situates himself within the movement engendering them: namely, the revolutionary movement. It is also an act because, once this philosophy is made explicit, it renders the militant more conscious of his destiny, his place in the world and his goals.

So revolutionary thinking is a *thinking in situation*: it is the thinking of the oppressed insofar as they rise up together against oppression. It cannot be reconstructed from outside. It can merely be learned, once it has been developed, by reproducing in oneself the revolutionary movement and viewing it from the standpoint of the situation from which it emanates. We should note that the thinking of philosophers from the ruling class also constitutes action, as Nizan has clearly shown in his book, *Les Chiens de garde*.[19] Its aim is to defend, conserve and repel. But its inferiority to revolutionary thinking comes from the fact that the philosophy of oppression seeks to hide its pragmatic character from itself. Since it aims not to change the world, but to keep it in being, it claims to *contemplate* the world as it *is*. It views society and nature from the standpoint of pure knowledge, without admitting to itself that this attitude tends to perpetuate the present state of the world by convincing us that it is easier to know it than to change it or, at least, that if we want to change it, we must first know it.

The theory of the primacy of knowledge exerts a negative, inhibiting effect by conferring a pure, static essence on things, unlike any philosophy of work which grasps the object through the action that modifies that object by using it. But it contains in itself a negation of the effect it exerts, since, precisely, it asserts the primacy of knowing and rejects any pragmatic conception of truth. The superiority of revolutionary thinking lies in the fact that it proclaims its character as action from the outset; it is conscious of being an act; and if it presents itself as a total understanding of the universe, that is because the project of the oppressed worker is a total attitude towards the universe as a whole. But since revolutionaries need to distinguish the true from the false, this indissoluble unity of thought and action calls for a new and systematic theory of truth. The pragmatic conception cannot meet their requirements, since it is subjectivist idealism pure and simple. This is why the materialist myth was invented. It has the advantage of reducing thought to being merely one of the forms of universal energy and thus divesting it of its wan, will-o'-the-wisp aspect. Moreover, it presents thought in each case as one objective behaviour among others; in other words, as something brought about by the state

201

of the world and reacting back on that state to modify
it. But we have just seen that the notion of a conditioned thinking collapses of itself; further on, I shall
demonstrate that the same applies to the notion of
determinate action. The point is not to create a cos-
mogonic myth to give symbolic representation to the
act of thought, but to abandon all myths and return
to the true revolutionary requirement which is that of
uniting action and truth, thought and realism. In a
word, we need a philosophical theory which shows
that human reality is action and that action on the
world is the same as the understanding of that world
as it is; which shows, in other words, that action is disclosure of reality *at the same time* as it is modification of
that reality.[20] But, as we have seen, the materialist myth
is, additionally, the figurative representation, within
the unity of a cosmology, of the movement of history, of the relation of human beings to matter and
the relation of human beings among themselves. It is,
in short, the figurative representation of all the revolutionary themes. We must go back, then, to the struc-
turing of the revolutionary attitude and examine it in
detail to see whether it calls only for a mythic figura-

tion or whether, by contrast, it calls for the ground-work of a rigorous philosophy.

Every member of the dominant class is a man of divine right. Born into a world of leaders, he is convinced from childhood that he is born *to command* and, in a sense, this is true because his parents have bred him to take over from them. There is a certain social function that awaits him in the future, a function into which he will slip as soon as he is old enough and which is akin to the metaphysical reality of his person. In his own eyes, then, he is a person, an a priori synthesis of fact and legal right. Awaited by his peers and destined to take over from them in due course, he exists because he *has the right* to exist. This sacred character of one bourgeois for another, which manifests itself in ceremonies of *recognition* (such as greetings, visiting cards, formal announcements, ritual visits, etc.), is what is called human dignity. The ideology of the ruling class is steeped in this idea of dignity. And when men are said to be 'the lords of creation', this should be understood in its most literal form: they are its divine-right monarchs; the world is made for them; their existence is the absolute value, perfectly satisfying to the mind, that gives the universe its meaning. This is what is originally meant in all the philosophical systems that assert the primacy of subject over object and the constitution of nature by the activity of thought. It is self-evident that, in these conditions, man is a supernatural being. What is called nature is the sum total of what exists without having the right to do so.

For the sacred individuals, the oppressed classes are part of nature. They must not command. Perhaps in other societies the fact of a slave's being born within the *domus* conferred a sacred character on him also: that of being born *to* serve; of being, over against the man of divine right, the man of divine duty. But in the case of the proletariat the same cannot be said. The worker's son, born in some outlying industrial district, living among the crowd, has no direct contact with the propertied elite. He has no personal duties other than those laid down by the law; he is not even forbidden, if he possesses that mysterious grace known as merit, to gain access, under certain circumstances and on certain conditions, to the upper class, at which point his son or grandson will become a man by divine right. In this way, he is simply a living being, the best organized of the

animals. Everyone has felt the contempt implicit in the
term 'natural' that is used to refer to the natives of a
colonial land. The banker, the industrialist or even the
teacher from the 'home country' are not the 'natural'
inhabitants of any country; they do not fall into this
natural category at all. By contrast, the oppressed person does: each of the events in his life tells him he is
not entitled to exist. His parents did not bring him into
the world for any particular end, but by chance and *for
nothing*. At best, it was because they loved children or
because they were susceptible to a certain kind of propaganda or because they wanted to enjoy the benefits
granted to large families. No special function awaits
him; and if he is apprenticed, this is not to prepare him
to exercise the priesthood of a profession but merely to
enable him to prolong the unjustifiable existence he has
been leading since his birth. He will work in order to
live, and to say the ownership of the fruits of his labour
will be stolen from him is an understatement: the very
meaning of his work is stolen from him, since he feels
himself no part of the society for which he produces.

Whether he is a fitter or a labourer, he knows very
well that he is not irreplaceable. Indeed, it is this inter-

changeability that characterizes the 'workers'. The work of the doctor or the lawyer is judged by its quality, that of the 'good' worker by its quantity alone. Through the circumstances of his situation he becomes aware of himself as a member of a zoological species: the human species. So long as he remains on this level, his condition itself seems natural to him: he will carry on his life as he began it, with sudden revolts if oppression bears down on him more strongly, but these will be merely spontaneous.

The revolutionary transcends this situation because he wants to change it. And it is from the point of view of this will-to-change that he regards it. We must note, first of all, that he wants to change it for his whole class, not for himself. If he were thinking merely of himself he could, as we have seen, leave the terrain of the species and embrace the values of the dominant class. Self-evidently in that case he would accept a priori the sacred character of the men of divine right, for the sole purpose of benefitting from it in his turn. But, as he cannot envisage claiming that divine right for *his whole class*, since it originates precisely in an oppression he wishes to destroy, his first move will be to contest the rights of the ruling class. In his eyes, the men of divine right do not exist. He has not moved among them, but he senses that they lead an existence not unlike his own, equally vague and un-justifiable. Unlike the members of the oppressor class, he does not seek to exclude the members of the other class from the human community. But he wants, from the outset, to divest them of that magical aspect that makes them formidable for those whom they oppress. Moreover, a spontaneous impulse leads him to deny the values they have initially established. If it were true that theirs was an a priori Good, then revolution would be poisoned in its essence: to rise up against the oppressor class would be to rise up against Good in general. But his plan is not to replace this Good by another a priori Good, for he is not in the phase of construction: he merely wishes to free himself from all the values and rules of conduct the ruling class has devised because those values and rules are simply a brake on his activity and are, by their very nature, aimed at preserving the status quo. And since he wishes to change the way society is organized, he has first to reject the idea that it was ordained by

Providence: only if he regards it as a fact can he hope to replace it with another fact that suits him better.

At the same time, revolutionary thought is humanistic. The assertion that 'we too are human beings' underlies all revolutions. And, by this, the revolutionary means that his oppressors are human beings. He will, no doubt, do violence to them; he will attempt to throw off their yoke but, if he must destroy some of their lives, he will always try to keep this destruction to a minimum because he needs technicians and managers. So even the bloodiest of revolutions involves defections; it is, above all, an absorption and assimilation of the oppressor class by the oppressed class. By contrast with the turncoats or members of a persecuted minority who want to raise themselves to the level of the privileged and assimilate to them, revolutionaries want to bring them down to their level by denying the validity of their privileges. And, since the continual sense of their contingency inclines them to recognize themselves as unjustifiable facts, they regard the men of divine right as mere facts similar to themselves. Revolutionaries are not, then, people who claim rights but, rather, people who destroy the very notion of right, which they see as a product of custom and force. Their humanism is not based on human dignity, but denies human beings any particular dignity; the unity in which they wish to merge all their fellows and themselves is not that of the human realm, but of the human species. There is a human species, an unjustifiable, contingent phenomenon; the circumstances of its development have brought it to a kind of inner imbalance; the revolutionary's task is to make it find a more rational equilibrium beyond its present state. Just as the species has closed around the men of divine right and absorbed them, so nature closes around human beings and absorbs them: the human being is a natural fact; humanity is one species among others.

Only in this way does the revolutionary think he can escape the mystifications of the privileged class. The man who knows himself to be natural can never again be mystified by the recourse to a priori moralities. At this point materialism seems to offer him its aid; it is the epic of the factual. The links that form across the materialist world are no doubt necessary, but necessity appears here within an original contingency. If the universe exists, its development and successive states may be governed by laws. But it is not a *necessity* that the universe should exist, or that there should be Being in general, and the contingency of the universe communicates itself through all the connections—even the most rigorous ones—to each particular fact. Each state, governed from outside by the previous one, may be modified if one acts on its causes. And the new state is neither more nor less *natural* than the preceding one, if by this we mean that it is not based on rights and that its necessity is merely relative. At the same time, since it is a question of imprisoning man in the world, materialism possesses the advantage of offering a crude myth of the origin of species in which the most complex forms derive from the simplest. It is not a matter of replacing the end by the cause in each case, but of presenting a stereotyped image of a world in which causes have everywhere replaced ends. That materialism has always had this function can already be seen in the attitude of the first and most naïve of the great materialists: Epicurus recognizes that an endless number of different explanations could be as true as materialism. That is to say, they could account for the phenomena just as exactly.

But he defies us to find one that frees man from his fears more completely. And the essential fear of human beings, particularly where they are suffering, is not so much death or the existence of a harsh God, but simply that the state of affairs from which they are suffering was produced and is maintained for unknowable, transcendent ends. Any effort to modify it would then be futile and blameworthy. A subtle discouragement would insinuate itself right into their judgements and prevent them from wishing for, or even conceiving of, any improvement. Epicurus reduced death to a fact by removing from it the moral aspect it gained from the fiction of underworld seats of judgement. He did not eliminate ghosts, but he turned them into strictly physical phenomena. He did not dare eliminate the gods, but he reduced them to being merely a divine *species* unrelated to ourselves. He took from them the power to create themselves and showed they were produced, as we are, by the streaming of atoms.

But here again, though it may have been useful and encouraging, is the materialist myth really necessary? What the consciousness of the revolutionary demands is that the privileges of the oppressor class should be unjustifiable, that the original contingency he finds within himself should also be constitutive of the very existence of his oppressors and, lastly, that the system of values constructed by his masters, the aim of which is to confer a *de jure* existence on *de facto* advantages, can be supplanted by an as yet non-existent form of organization of the world that will exclude all privileges *de jure* and *de facto*. But he clearly has an ambivalent attitude to the *natural*. In a way, he plunges into nature, dragging his masters with him, but, on the other hand, he declares that he wishes to substitute a rational scheme of human relations for the combination blindly produced by nature.

The expression Marxism uses to refer to the future society is *antiphysis*. This means that the aim is to establish a human order whose laws will be the negation of natural laws. And doubtless we are meant to understand that this order will be produced only by first obeying the prescriptions of nature. But, ultimately, the fact is that this order must be *conceived* within the nature that denies it; the fact is that, in the anti-natural society, the representation of the law will precede the establishment of the law, instead of the law conditioning the representation we have of it, as, according to materialism, it does today.

In short, the transition to *antiphysis* signifies the replacement of the society of laws by the community of ends. And, without a doubt, the revolutionary distrusts values and refuses to acknowledge that he is pursuing a better organization of the human community: he fears that a return to values, even by a detour, may open the door to new mystifications. But, on the other hand, the mere fact that he is willing to sacrifice his life for an order that he never expects to see arrive implies that that future order, which justifies all his acts but which he will not enjoy, functions for him as a value. What is a value if not the call of that which does not yet exist?[21]

In order to meet these various demands, a revolutionary philosophy should set aside the materialist myth and attempt to show: (1) that man is unjustifiable; that his existence is contingent insofar as neither he nor any Providence has produced it; (2) in consequence, that any collective order established by human beings may be transcended in the direction of other orders; (3) that the value system in force in a society reflects the structure of that society and tends to preserve it; (4) that it may, therefore, always be transcended in the direction of other systems, which are not clearly perceived, since the society they will express does not exist yet, but are foreshadowed and, all in all, invented by the very efforts of the members of the society to transcend that society. The oppressed person lives out his original contingency, and revolutionary philosophy must take account of this. But, in living out his contingency, he accepts the right to existence of his oppressors and the absolute value of the ideologies they have produced. He becomes a revolutionary only by a movement of transcendence that throws those rights and ideologies into question.

Revolutionary philosophy has, above all, to explain the possibility of this movement of transcendence. It is clear that it cannot derive its source from the purely material, natural existence of the individual, since it looks back over that existence to judge it from the standpoint of the future. This possibility of *rising above* a situation to gain a vantage point on it (a vantage point that is not pure knowledge but is, inseparably, both understanding and action) is precisely what we call freedom. No kind of materialism will ever explain it. A sequence of causes and effects may well induce from me an action or a course of behaviour which will itself be an effect and will modify the state of the world. It cannot make me look back on my situation to grasp it in its totality. In a word, it cannot account for revolutionary class consciousness. The materialist dialectic is no doubt there to explain and justify this transcendence in the direction of the future. But it works to lodge freedom in things, not in human beings, which is absurd. A state of the world will never be able to produce class consciousness.

Marxists know this so well that they rely on militants—that is to say on conscious, concerted action—to radicalize the masses and arouse this consciousness in them. This is all very well, but where do these militants find their understanding of the situation? Must they not, at some point or other, have risen above the situation, or stepped back from it? Lastly, to avoid the revolutionary's being mystified by his former masters, he has to be shown that established values are mere facts. But if they are facts and, as a result, capable of being transcended, this is not because they are values but because they are something established. And to avoid his mystifying himself, he has to be given the means of understanding that the goal he is pursuing—whether he calls it *antiphysis*, the classless society or the liberation of man—is also a value; and if there is no way of going beyond this value, that is only because it has not yet been realized. This is what Marx sensed when he spoke of going beyond Communism, and Trotsky when he talked of permanent revolution. A contingent, unjustifiable, but free being, wholly immersed in a society that oppresses him, but capable of transcending that society by his efforts to change it—this is what the revolutionary human being demands to be. Idealism mystifies him by tying him up with already established rights and values; it conceals from him his power to invent his own path. But materialism also mystifies him, by robbing him of his freedom. Revolutionary philosophy must be a philosophy of transcendence.

But, all sophistry apart, the revolutionary himself mistrusts freedom. And he is right to do so. There has never been any lack of prophets to tell him he is free, and in each case it was to dupe him. Stoic freedom, Christian freedom and Bergsonian freedom have merely strengthened his chains by concealing them. They were all reducible to a certain *inner* freedom that human beings could preserve in any situation. This inner freedom is a pure idealist mystification: care is taken not to present it as the necessary condition for *action*. It is, in fact, pure enjoyment of itself. If Epictetus in chains does not rebel, that is because he feels free, he enjoys his freedom. But on this basis, one state of affairs is as good as another; the slave is as free as the master; why wish for change?

Ultimately, this freedom is reducible to a more or less clear assertion of the autonomy of thought. But in conferring independence on thought, it separates it from the situation (since truth is universal, one may think truth in any situation whatever) and separates it also from action (since the intention alone depends on us, the act, in being performed, undergoes pressure from the world's real forces, which distort it and render it unrecognizable to its very perpetrator). Abstract thoughts and empty intentions are all that are left to the slave in the name of metaphysical freedom.

217

And, meanwhile, his masters' orders or the need to make a living have committed him to harsh, concrete actions, and compel him to form detailed thoughts about matter and tools.

The liberating element for the oppressed individual is, in fact, work. In this sense, it is initially work that is revolutionary. Admittedly, that work is *done to order* and appears initially as the subjugation of the worker. It is improbable that he would have chosen to do *this* work in *these* conditions and in *this* time span for *this* pay if he had not been compelled to. More rigorous than the master of ancient times, the employer goes so far as to determine in advance the actions and behaviour of the worker. He breaks down the worker's act into elements, takes some of these away to have them done by other workers and reduces the conscious, synthetic activity to a mere sum of indefinitely repeated movements. In this way, by assimilating the worker's actions to properties, he tends to reduce him to the state of a thing, pure and simple. Mme de Staël cites a striking example of such a reduction in her account of the journey she made to Russia in the early nineteenth century: 'Out of twenty musicians (of a band of Russian serfs), each one plays one single note each time it recurs. As a result, each of these men bears the name of the note he is responsible for sounding. As they go by, one hears, "There is Mr Nar-ishkine's G, E or D".' Here, then, is the individual lim-ited to a constant property that defines him, like an atomic weight or a melting point. Modern Taylorism does just this. The worker becomes the man of a sin-gle operation, which he repeats a hundred times a day. He is merely an object and it would be childish or des-picable to tell a shoe-stitcher or the worker who puts the needles in the speedometers of Ford cars that, amid the action they are involved in, they retain their inner freedom of thought. But at the same time, work offers the beginnings of a concrete liberation, even in these extreme cases, because it is, first, the negation of the contingent, capricious order that is the master's order. At work, the oppressed individual is no longer concerned to please the master; he escapes the world of the dance-band, of politeness, ceremony and psychology; he does not have to guess what is going on in the boss's head; he is no longer at the mercy of someone's mood. His work is, admittedly, imposed on him at the outset and the fruits of his labours are stolen from him at the end. But within these two limits, his work confers on him a mastery of things; the worker apprehends himself as the possibility of infinitely varying the form of a material object by acting upon it in accordance with certain universal rules. In other words, it is the determinism of matter that offers him the first image of his freedom.

A worker is not deterministic in the way a scientist is. He does not subscribe to determinism as an explicitly formulated postulate. He lives it in his gestures, in the movement of an arm striking a rivet or lowering a lever. He is so steeped in determinism that, when the desired effect is not produced, he will try to find what hidden cause has prevented it from occurring, without ever supposing any waywardness in things or any sudden, contingent breakdown in the natural order. And since it is at the deepest point of his slavery, at the very moment the master's whim transforms him into a thing, that his action liberates him by conferring on him the government of things and a specialist's autonomy the master cannot infringe, the idea of liberation has become combined in his mind with that of determinism. He cannot, in fact, apprehend freedom as something floating above the world, since, for the master or the oppressor class he is, precisely, a thing. He does not learn that he is free by looking back reflexively upon himself but, rather, transcends his slavish state by his action on phenomena which, by the very rigorousness with which they are connected, reflect back to him the image of a concrete freedom: namely, his freedom to modify them. And since the beginnings of his concrete freedom appear to him in the links of determinism, it is no surprise that he aims to replace the relation of man to man, which seems to him the relation of a tyrannical freedom to a humiliated obedience, with a relation of man to thing; and finally, from another standpoint—since the man who governs things is in turn a thing—by a relation of thing to thing.

Hence, determinism—insofar as it stands opposed to the psychology of civility—looks to him like a purifying form of thought, a catharsis. And if he looks back at himself to regard himself as a determinate thing, he thereby liberates himself from the formidable freedom of his masters, as he sweeps them up with him into the connecting links of determinism and regards them in their turn as things, by explaining their orders in terms of their situation, instincts and history—that is, by immersing them in the world. If all men are things, there are no longer any slaves; there are only the *de facto* oppressed. Like Samson, who consented to be buried beneath the ruins of the temple, provided that the Philistines perished with him, the slave frees himself by eliminating the freedom of his masters with his own and being engulfed, alongside them, in matter. The liberated society of his conceiving is the opposite of Kant's community of ends; it is not based on the reciprocal recognition of freedoms. But, since the liberating relationship is that between man and things, that is what will constitute the basic structure of this society. The relation of oppression between men has merely to be eliminated for the wills of both slave and master, worn down by reciprocal struggle, to be entirely redirected towards things. Liberated society will be a harmonious enterprise of exploitation of the world. As it is produced by the absorption of the privileged classes and is defined by work or, in other words, by action on matter and, as

it is itself subject to the laws of determinism, the circle is closed and the world is rounded off once more.
Unlike the rebel, the revolutionary wants an *order*. And
since the spiritual orders he is offered are always more
or less the mystifying image of the society oppressing
him, it is the material order he will choose—that is to
say, the order of effectiveness, in which he will figure
both as cause and effect. Here again, materialism offers itself. The materialist myth offers the most exact
image of a society in which freedoms are alienated.

Auguste Comte defined it as the doctrine that
seeks to explain the higher in terms of the lower. Naturally, the terms 'higher' and 'lower' are not to be
taken in a moral sense here, but refer to more or less
complicated forms of organization. Now, it is precisely the case that the worker is regarded by the person he feeds and protects as an inferior, and the
oppressor class takes itself originally for the upper
class. By dint of the fact that its internal structures are
more complex and refined, it is that class which
produces ideologies, culture and value systems. The
tendency of the upper strata of society is to explain
the lower in terms of the higher, either by regarding

the lower as a debasement of the higher or by taking the view that it exists *in order to* serve the needs of the higher. This type of teleological explanation is, naturally, elevated into a general principle for interpreting the universe. By contrast, the explanation 'from below'—that is to say, in terms of economic, technical and ultimately biological conditioning—is the one the oppressed adopt, because it makes them the foundation of the whole society. If the higher is merely an emanation of the lower, then the 'exquisite class' is merely an epiphenomenon. If the oppressed refuse to serve it, it withers and dies; by itself it is nothing. One has only to expand this—correct—conception and turn it into a general explanatory principle for materialism to be born. And the materialist explanation of the universe—that is, of the biological by the physico-chemical and of thought by matter—becomes in its turn a justification of the revolutionary attitude; by creating a structured myth, this explanation turns a spontaneous stirring of revolt of the oppressed against their oppressor into a universal mode of existence of reality.

Here again, materialism gives the revolutionary more than he asks for. For the revolutionary asks to

govern things, not to be one. Admittedly, he has acquired from his work a proper estimation of freedom.
The freedom reflected back to him by his action on
things is far removed from the Stoic's abstract freedom of thought. It manifests itself in a particular situation, into which the worker has been thrown by the
chance of his birth and by the whim or self-interest of
his master. It appears within an undertaking that he
did not begin of his own free will and that he will not
finish; it cannot be distinguished from his very engagement within that undertaking; but ultimately if,
in the very depths of his slavery, he becomes aware of
his freedom, this is because he can gauge the effectiveness of his concrete action. He does not possess
the pure idea of an autonomy that he does not enjoy
but he knows his power, which is proportionate to his
action. What he finds, during the action itself, is that
he transcends the present state of matter through a
precise plan for arranging it in a particular way and
since that plan is identical with the government-of-
means-with-a-view-to-ends, he succeeds in fact in arranging it as he wanted. If he discovers the relation
of cause and effect, he does so not by suffering it but
in the very act that transcends the present state (the

adherence of coal to the walls of the mine, etc.) in the direction of a certain goal that casts light on and, from the depths of the future, defines that state. So the causal relation discloses itself in and through the efficacy of an act that is both project and realization.

It is the tractability and, with it, the resistance of the universe that reflect back to him at one and the same time both the constancy of causal series and the image of his freedom, but that is because his freedom is indistinguishable from the use of causal series for an end that it sets itself. Without the light that end casts on the present situation, there would be neither causal relation nor means–ends relationship in this situation; or, rather, there would be an indistinct infinity of means and ends, effects and causes, the way there would be an undifferentiated infinity of circles, ellipses, triangles and polygons, were it not for the generative act of the mathematician who draws a particular figure by linking a series of points selected in terms of some law. Thus, in the performance of work, determinism does not reveal freedom insofar as it is an abstract law of nature, but only insofar as a human project carves out and throws light on a certain partial determinism amid the infinite interaction of phenomena. And in this determinism, which finds its proof simply in the efficacy of human action—in much the same way as Archimedes' Principle was already in use and understood by shipbuilders long before Archimedes gave it its conceptual form—the relationship of cause to effect is indistinguishable from that of means to end.

The organic unity of the worker's project consists in the simultaneous emergence of an end that was not originally in the universe, which manifests itself through the disposition of means for achieving it (for the end is nothing other than the synthetic unity of all the means brought together to produce it). At the same time, the undergirding for these means, which reveals itself in turn in their very disposition, is the relation of cause and effect: like Archimedes' Principle, which was both the underpinning and the content of the shipbuilders' technique. In this sense, we may say that the atom is created by the atomic bomb, which is conceivable only in the light of the Anglo-American project of winning a war. Thus, freedom is discovered only in the act, is indivisible from the act; it is the foundation of the connections and interac-

tions that form the internal structures of the act; it is
never mere self-enjoyment, but reveals itself in and
through its products; it is not an inner virtue that gives
one licence to detach oneself from the most urgent
situations, since, for human beings, there is neither
outside nor inside. It is, rather, the power to commit
oneself to present action and to build a future; it generates a future that enables us to understand and
change the present. So the worker actually learns his
freedom through things: but precisely because things
teach him his freedom, he is anything but a thing. And
it is here that materialism mystifies him and becomes,
in spite of itself, an instrument in the hands of the
oppressors: for if the worker discovers his freedom
in his work, conceived as the original relation of man
to material things, he thinks of himself as a thing in
his relations with the master who oppresses him; it is
the master who, in reducing him through Taylorism
or any other procedure, to be merely an ever-identical
sum of operations, transforms him into a passive object, the mere medium of constant properties.

Materialism, by breaking man down into units of
behaviour conceived strictly along the lines of Tay-

lorist operations, plays the master's game; it is the master who conceives the slave as a machine; by regarding himself as a mere product of nature, as a 'natural being', the slave sees himself *through the master's eyes*. He conceives himself as an Other and with the thoughts of the Other. There is a unity between the materialist revolutionary's conception and that of his oppressors. Now, doubtless it will be said that the result of materialism is to catch the master and transform him into a thing like the slave. But the master knows nothing of this and cares less: he lives within his ideologies, rights and culture. It is only to the subjectivity of the slave that he appears as a thing. It is, therefore, infinitely more useful and true to allow the slave to discover through his work his freedom to change the world and, consequently, to change his own state, than to go to enormous lengths, by concealing his true freedom from him, to demonstrate to him that his master is a thing. And, if it is true that materialism, as an explanation of the higher by the lower, is an appropriate picture of the current structure of our society, it is simply all the more obvious that this is merely a myth in the Platonic sense of the term. For the revolutionary has no concern for a symbolic expression of the present situation; he wants a form of thought that will enable him to forge the future. And the fact is that the materialist myth will lose all meaning in a classless society in which there will no longer be either higher or lower.

But, say the Marxists, if you teach man he *is* free, you betray him since he then no longer needs to *become* so. Can you imagine a freeborn man demanding his liberation? To which I reply that if man is not originally free, but determined once and for all, you cannot even conceive what his liberation might mean. Some tell me, 'we shall divest human nature of the constraints that deform it.' Such people are fools. What can a man's nature be apart from what he is concretely in his present existence? How could a Marxist believe in a *true* human nature that would merely be masked by the circumstances of oppression? Others claim they are bringing about human happiness. But what is a happiness that would not be *felt* and *experienced*? Happiness is, in its essence, subjectivity. How could it survive under the reign of objectivity?

230

The only outcome one can really hope to achieve, assuming universal determinism and taking the viewpoint of objectivity, is a more rational organization of society, but what value can such an organization retain if it is not experienced as such by a free subjectivity and transcended in the direction of new ends. There is, in fact, no opposition between these two demands of action—namely, that the agent should be free and the world in which he acts should be determined. For it is not from the same standpoint or in relation to the same realities that one subscribes to the two: freedom is a structure of human action and appears only in commitment [*engagement*]; determinism is the law of the world. Moreover, action demands only partial linkages and local constants.

In the same way, it is not true that a free man cannot wish to be liberated. For it is not in the same respects that he is free and in chains. His freedom is, as it were, the illumination of the situation into which he is thrown. But the freedom of others may make the situation untenable for him, may drive him to revolt or death. Though the work of slaves manifests their freedom, that work is, nonetheless, imposed, crushing and corrosive; the fruits of their labours are spirited away from them; they are isolated by their work, excluded from a society that exploits them and with which they feel no solidarity, pressed up as they are against matter by a *vis a tergo*. It is the case that they are merely links in a chain of which they know neither the beginning nor the end; it is true that the master's gaze, his ideology and his commands tend to deny them any existence other than the material. It is precisely by becoming revolutionaries, that is, by organizing the other members of their class to reject the tyranny of their masters, that they will best manifest their freedom. Oppression leaves them no choice but resignation or revolution. But, in each case, they manifest their freedom to choose. And, lastly, whatever goal is assigned to the revolutionary, he goes beyond it and sees it merely as one stage. If he seeks security or a better material organization of society, it is in order that they may serve him as a point of departure.

This was the Marxists' own reply when, in response to some minor wage-claim, reactionaries spoke of the 'sordid materialism of the masses'. They gave it to be understood that behind these material demands there was the assertion of a humanism, that these workers were not just calling for a few shillings more but that their demand was, so to speak, the concrete symbol of their need to be treated as human beings. Human beings, that is to say, freedoms in possession of their own destiny.[22] This remark is valid so far as the revolutionary's ultimate goal is concerned. Beyond the rational organization of the community, class consciousness calls for a new humanism; it is an alienated freedom that has taken freedom as its goal. Socialism is simply the means that will enable the reign of freedom to be achieved; a materialist socialism is, therefore, contradictory, because socialism sets as its goal a humanism that materialism renders inconceivable.

A feature of idealism that particularly disgusts the revolutionary is the tendency to represent changes in the world as governed by ideas or, better, as changes in ideas. Death, unemployment, poverty, hunger and the suppression of strikes are not ideas. They are everyday realities that are experienced with abhorrence. They doubtless have a meaning, but they retain, above all, a basic irrational opacity. The 1914 war was

not, as Louis Chevalier said, 'Descartes against Kant';
it was the inexpiable deaths of twelve million young
men. The revolutionary, crushed beneath reality, refuses to let it be conjured away. He knows the revolution will not be a mere consumption of ideas, but that
it will cost blood, sweat and human lives. It is his business to know that things are solid and can, at times,
pose insuperable obstacles, that the best-conceived
project encounters resistances that sometimes make
it fail. He knows action is not a happy combination
of ideas, but a whole man's effort against the stubborn
impenetrability of the universe. He knows that, when
the meanings of things have been deciphered, there
remains an unassimilable residue—the otherness, irra-
tionality and opaqueness of the real—and that it is
this residue that eventually stifles and crushes. Unlike
the idealist, whose sloppy thinking he condemns, he
sees himself as hard-headed. More than this, against
the countervailing power of things he wants to pit not
ideas but that action that ultimately involves effort,
exhausting fatigue and sleepless nights.

Here again, materialism seems to offer him the
most satisfying expression of his demand since it as-

serts the predominance of impenetrable matter over ideas. For materialism, all is fact, conflicts of forces, action. Thought itself becomes a real phenomenon in a measurable world; it is produced by matter and consumes energy. It is in terms of realism that the famous pre-eminence of the object must be conceived. But is this interpretation so deeply satisfying? Does it not overshoot its aim and mystify the demand that gave birth to it? If it is true that nothing seems less like effort than the generation of ideas one by another, effort vanishes just as quickly if we regard the universe as a balance of diverse forces. Nothing gives less of an impression of effort than a force applied to a material point: it does the work of which it is capable, no more and no less, and transforms itself mechanically into kinetic or calorific energy. Nowhere and in no case does nature of itself give us the impression of resistance overcome, of revolt and submission, of weariness. In every circumstance it is everything it can be and that is all. And opposing forces are reconciled, in accordance with the serene laws of mechanics. For reality to be described as a resistance to be overcome by work, that resistance has to be experienced by a subjectivity seeking to conquer it. Nature conceived as pure objectivity is the opposite of the idea. But, precisely on that account, it transforms itself into an idea; it is the pure idea of objectivity. The *real* vanishes. For the real is what is impermeable to a *subjectivity*: it is this lump of sugar which, as Bergson says, I must wait to see melt, or, if you prefer, it is the subject's obligation to experience such a wait. It is the human project; it is my thirst which determines that it 'takes a long time' to melt. Outside of human concerns, it melts neither slowly nor quickly but precisely in a time that depends on its nature, its density and the quantity of water in which it is soaking.

It is human subjectivity that discovers the *adversity* of the real in and through the project it forms of transcending it in the direction of the future. For a hill to be easy or hard to climb, someone has to have formed the project of ascending it. Idealism and materialism both make the real disappear, the one because it eliminates the thing, the other because it eliminates subjectivity. For reality to reveal itself, a human being has to struggle against it. In a word, the revolutionary's realism requires the existence both of the world and of

subjectivity. More than this, it requires such a correla
tion between the two that one cannot conceive a subjectivity apart from the world or a world that would
not be illuminated by the effort of a subjectivity.[23] The
maximum reality, the maximum resistance will be ob-
tained if we assume that human beings are by definition in-situation-in-the-world and that they learn the
difficult lesson of reality by defining themselves in
relation to it.

Let us note here, in fact, that too close an adherence to universal determinism runs the risk of eliminating any *resistance* on the part of reality. This was
proved to me in a conversation with M. Garaudy and
two of his comrades. I asked them if matters really
were cut and dried when Stalin signed the Russo- German Pact and when the French Communists decided to
participate in de Gaulle's government; I wondered
whether those responsible had not *run risks* with these
decisions, feeling rather anxious about their responsi-
bilities. For it seems to me that the chief characteristic
of reality is that we are never on totally firm ground
with it and the consequences of our acts are merely
probable. But M. Garaudy interrupted me: for him,

matters are cut and dried in advance; there is a science of history and the facts follow in a strict sequence. One is therefore making a safe bet. He was so carried away by his zeal that he ended up saying excitedly, 'And what does Stalin's intelligence matter? I don't give a fig for it!' It must be added that, under the stern glances of his comrades, he blushed, lowered his eyes and added with quite a pious air, 'though Stalin is very intelligent.'

Unlike revolutionary realism, then, which states that the least little result is achieved only with difficulty, amid the greatest uncertainty, the materialist myth leads some to be profoundly reassured about the outcome of their efforts. As they see it, they cannot but succeed. History is a science, its findings are written down, one has only to read them. This attitude is quite patently escapist. The revolutionary has overturned the bourgeois myths and the working class has undertaken, through a thousand vicissitudes, through snubs and climb-downs, victories and defeats, to forge its own destiny in freedom and in anguish. But our Garaudys are afraid. What they look for in Communism is not liberation, but a heightened discipline.

They fear nothing so much as freedom. And if they have thrown off the a priori values of the class from which they came, they have done so only to recover a prioris of knowledge and paths already marked out in history. There are no risks, no worries. All is safe, the outcomes are assured. As a result, reality vanishes and history is reduced to an idea unfolding itself.

Inside this idea, M. Garaudy feels safe. Communist intellectuals to whom I reported this conversation shrugged their shoulders; 'Garaudy is a scientist,' they informed me contemptuously. 'He is a Protestant bourgeois who, for his own edification, has replaced the finger of God with historical materialism.' I am quite willing to accept this and I will admit too that M. Garaudy didn't seem to me to be a shining light. But he writes a lot and the Communists do not disown him. And it is no accident that most scientists have found a home in the Communist Party and that that party, so severe on heresy, does not condemn them.

We must repeat the point here: if revolutionaries wish to act, they cannot regard historical events as the outcome of arbitrary contingencies. But they do not in any sense demand that the road be preordained for

239

them. On the contrary, they wish to find it for themselves. Some constants, certain partial series and structural laws within determinate social forms are what they need to do their planning. If you give them more, everything vanishes into ideas: history no longer has to be *made*, but can merely be *read off* day by day; the real becomes a dream.

We were enjoined to choose between materialism and idealism, and we were told we would be able to find no middle way between the two doctrines. We have allowed the exigencies of revolution to speak without preconceived ideas and we have found that these themselves marked out the lineaments of an original philosophy that rejects both idealism and materialism. It emerged for us, first, that the revolutionary act was the free act *par excellence*. Not with an anarchistic, individualist freedom; if that were the case, then the revolutionary, by his very situation, could only demand, more or less explicitly, the rights of the 'exquisite class', or, in other words, his integration into the upper social strata. But since he calls from within the oppressed class—and for the whole of it—for a more rational social status, his freedom lies in the act by which he demands the liberation of all his class and, more generally, of all human beings. It is, at its source, a recognition of other freedoms, and it demands to be recognized by them. Thus it places itself, from the outset, on the footing of solidarity. And the revolutionary act contains within itself the premises of a philosophy of freedom or, rather, by its very existence, creates that philosophy. But as, at the same time, the revolutionary discovers himself by and in his free project, as an oppressed person within an oppressed class, his original position requires that his *oppression* be explained to him. This means once again that human beings are free—for there can be no oppression of matter by matter, merely a balance of forces—and that a certain relationship may exist between freedoms, such that the one does not recognize the other and acts from outside it to transform it into an *object*. And reciprocally, since oppressed freedom seeks to liberate itself by force, the revolutionary attitude demands a theory of violence as a riposte to oppression. Here too, materialist terms are as inadequate for explaining violence as the conceptions of idealism.

Idealism, which is a philosophy of digestion and assimilation, does not even conceive the absolute, insurmountable pluralism of freedoms pitted one against another: idealism is a monism. But materialism is also a monism: there is no 'battle of opposites' within material unity. To tell the truth, there aren't even any opposites: hot and cold are merely different degrees on the thermometric scale; we pass progressively from light to darkness. Two equal and opposing forces cancel each other out and produce merely a state of equilibrium. The idea of a battle of opposites is the projection of human relationships on to material ones.

A revolutionary philosophy must account for the plurality of freedoms and show how each, while being a freedom for itself, must at the same time be able to be an object for others. Only this twofold character of freedom and objectivity can explain the complex notions of oppression, struggle, failure and violence. For it is only ever a freedom that is oppressed, but it can be oppressed only if it lends itself in some way to oppression; that is to say, if it presents the outward appearance of a thing to the Other. The revolutionary movement and its project, which is to take society by violence from a state in which freedoms are alienated to another state based on the mutual recognition of those freedoms, is to be understood in these terms.

Similarly, the revolutionary who *experiences* oppression bodily and in every one of his actions, in no way wishes to either underestimate the yoke under which he labours or tolerate idealist criticism dissipating that yoke into ideas. At the same time, he contests the rights of the privileged class and thereby destroys the idea of rights in general. But it would be a mistake to believe, as the materialist does, that he does so in order to replace them by *facts*, plain and simple. For facts can generate only facts, not representations of facts; the present generates another present, not the future. So the revolutionary act requires that the opposition between materialism—which can account for the disintegration of a society, but not the *construction* of a new one—and idealism—which confers a *de jure* existence on facts—be transcended in the unity of a synthesis. It calls for a new philosophy that takes a different view of human relations with the world.

If revolution is to be possible, human beings must be as contingent as facts; and yet they must differ from facts by their practical power to prepare the future and, consequently, to go beyond the present, to rise above their situation. This 'rising-above' is not in any sense comparable to the negative movement by which the Stoic attempts to take refuge within himself; it is by projecting themselves forward, by committing themselves to undertakings, that revolutionaries transcend the present. And since they are human beings acting like human beings, we must attribute to *all human activity* this ability to 'rise above'. The slightest human gesture is to be understood in terms of the future; even the reactionary is oriented towards the future, since his concern is to prepare a future identical to the past.

The absolute realism of the tactician demands that human beings be immersed in the real, threatened by concrete dangers, victims of concrete oppression from which they will free themselves by equally concrete action. Blood, sweat, pain and death are not ideas; the rock that crushes, the bullet that kills are not ideas. But for things to reveal what Bachelard rightly calls their 'coefficient of adversity', it takes the light of a project that illuminates them, be it merely the very simple and rudimentary one of living. It is untrue, then, as the idealist contends, that man is outside the world and nature, or that, like a reluctant bather, he has only dipped into it, keeping his head in a nobler air. He is entirely in the clutches of nature, which can crush him at any moment and destroy him body and soul. He is in nature's clutches from the very beginning: to be born really does mean 'coming into the world' in a situation not of his own choosing, with *this* body, *this* family and perhaps also *this* race. But if he does, indeed, plan to 'change the world', as Marx expressly states, that means he is originally a being for whom the world exists in its totality; this is something a lump of phosphorus or lead will never be, being merely a *part* of the world, played upon by forces to which it uncomprehendingly submits. This is because he transcends the world in the direction of a future state from which he can contemplate it, for it is by changing the world that we are able to know it. Neither the detached consciousness that would soar above the universe without being able to achieve a standpoint on it, nor the material object, which reflects a state of the world without comprehending it, can ever 'grasp' the totality of the existent in a synthesis—even a purely conceptual one. Only a human being in situation in the universe can do this, entirely weighed down as he is by the forces of nature, but transcending those forces totally by his project of harnessing them.

It is these new notions of 'situation' and 'being-in-the-world' which the revolutionary demands concretely, by the whole of his behaviour, to have elucidated. And if he escapes from the thickets of rights and duties into which the idealist attempts to mislead him, it should not be simply to fall into defiles narrowly marked out for him by the materialist. No doubt intelligent Marxists do acknowledge a certain contingency in history, but only to say that, if socialism fails, humanity will sink into barbarism. In short, if the constructive forces are to win out, historical determinism assigns them only one path. But there may be many kinds of barbarism and many socialisms—and perhaps even a barbaric socialism. What the revolutionary calls for is the possibility of human beings inventing their own law. This is the basis of his humanism and his socialism. Deep down, he does not

think—at least in his unmystified moments—that socialism is waiting for him just around history's corner,
like a robber with a cudgel in some corner of the
woods. He believes socialism is something he is *making* and, having shaken off all rights and dashed them
to the ground, he grants socialism no other entitlement to existence than the *fact* that the revolutionary
class invents it, wants it and will build it. Hence, the
slow, ruthless conquest of socialism is nothing other
than the affirmation, in and through history, of
human freedom. And precisely because man is free,
the triumph of socialism is not certain at all. It does
not stand at the end of the road, like some milestone,
but is *the* human project. It will be what human beings
make it; this is what emerges from the gravity with
which the revolutionary contemplates his action. He
not only feels responsible for the coming of a socialist
republic in general, but for the particular nature of
that socialism.

Thus revolutionary philosophy, transcending both
the idealist thinking that is bourgeois and the materialist
myth that suited the oppressed masses for a time, aspires to be the philosophy of *humanity* in general. And

it is quite natural that it should: if it is to be true, it will, in fact, be universal. The ambiguity of materialism is that it claims at times to be a class ideology and, at others, to be the expression of absolute truth. But the revolutionary, in his very choice of revolution, takes a privileged position: he does not fight for the preservation of a class, like the activist in the bourgeois parties, but for the elimination of classes; he does not divide society into men by divine right and natural men or *Untermenschen*, but calls for the unification of ethnic groups and classes—in a word, for the unity of *all human beings*; he does not allow himself to be mystified by rights and duties lodged a priori in an intelligible heaven, but posits, in the very act of revolt against them, human freedom, metaphysical and entire; he is the human being who wishes human beings to assume their destiny freely and totally. So his cause is essentially the cause of humanity and his philosophy must speak the *truth* about humanity.

But, you will say, if it is universal, that is to say, true for all, is it not by that same token beyond parties and classes? Are we not back with apolitical, asocial, rootless idealism? My answer is that this philosophy can reveal itself, at first, only to revolutionaries or, in other words, to people who are *in the situation of oppressed persons*, and that it needs them to manifest itself in the world. But it is true that it must be able to be the philosophy of every human being, insofar as a bourgeois oppressor is himself oppressed by his own oppression. For, to keep the oppressed classes under his rule, he must pay with his own person and become enmeshed in the tangle of rights and duties he has invented.

If the revolutionary retains the materialist myth, the young bourgeois can come to the revolution only through the perception of social injustices; he comes to it out of individual generosity, which is always suspect, since the source of generosity may dry up, and he faces the additional ordeal of swallowing a materialism that is inimical to his reason and that does not express his personal situation. But if the revolutionary philosophy is once made explicit, the bourgeois who has criticized the ideology of his class, who has recognized his contingency and freedom, who has understood that that freedom can be asserted only through the *recognition* bestowed on it by other freedoms, will discover that

249

this philosophy speaks to him of himself, insofar as he wishes to strip away the mystifying apparatus of the bourgeois class and assert himself as a human being among others. At that point, revolutionary humanism will not appear to him as the philosophy of an oppressed class but as the Truth itself—the truth humiliated, masked, oppressed by human beings whose interests lie in flight from it. And it will become manifest to all persons of goodwill that it is truth that is revolutionary. Not the abstract Truth of idealism, but the concrete truth—the truth willed, created, maintained and won through social struggle by human beings working for the liberation of humanity.

It will perhaps be objected that this analysis of revolutionary demands is abstract, since ultimately the only existing revolutionaries are Marxists and they subscribe to materialism. It is true that the Communist Party is the only revolutionary party. And it is true that materialism is the Party's doctrine. But I have not been attempting to describe what Marxists *believe*, but to tease out the implications of what it is that they *do*. And frequenting Communists has taught me that nothing is more variable, abstract and subjective than what is termed their Marxism. What could be more different from M. Garaudy's naïve, stubborn scientism than M. Hervé's philosophy? You may say that difference reflects the difference in their intelligences and this is true. But, above all, it indicates the degree of awareness each has of his deep attitude and the degree to which each believes in the materialist myth. It is not by accident that there is said to be a crisis in Marxist thinking today and that Marxism is resigned to having people like Garaudy as its spokesmen. The Communists are caught between the obsolescence of the materialist myth and the fear of introducing division, or at least hesitation, into their ranks by adopting a new ideology.

The best have fallen silent; the silence has been filled up with the chatter of imbeciles. 'After all,' the leaders no doubt think, 'what does ideology matter? Our old ideology has proved its worth and will no doubt lead us to victory. Our struggle isn't about ideas: it is a political and social struggle between human beings.' No doubt they are right so far as the present and the near future are concerned. But what kind of human beings will they make? You cannot get away with training generations of human beings by teaching them errors that happen to work. What will happen if one day materialism suffocates the revolutionary project?

Les Temps modernes, June 1946.

Notes

1   As I have been unfairly charged with not quoting Marx in this article, I should like to point out that my criticisms are not directed against him, but against the Marxist scholasticism of 1949. Or, if one prefers, against Marx *through* Stalinist neo-Marxism.

2   Karl Marx and Friedrich Engels, *Complete Works* (New York: International Publishers, 1980), VOL. 14, p. 651. I quote this text for the use that is being made of it *today*. I propose to demonstrate elsewhere that Marx had a much deeper and richer conception of objectivity.

3   Hegel's exact words seem to have been: '*Der Geist ist ein Knochen*'—spirit is a bone. [Trans.]

4   Friedrich Engels, *Socialism, Utopian and Scientific*,

Chapter 2, 'Dialectics' (New York: International Publishers, 1972), p. 48.

5   Ibid.

6   Sartre does not reference this passage, which is from *The Dialectics of Nature* (1940). Following Engels, he also fails to note that the words from 'For example . . .' onwards are from Section 108 of Hegel's *Logic* (Oxford: Clarendon, 1978, pp. 158–9), though the translation differs slightly. [Trans.]

7   There is no way out of this problem by speaking of intensive quantities. Bergson long ago exposed the confusions and errors in this myth that was the undoing of the psycho-physicists. Temperature, insofar as it is felt by us, is a quality. It is not *hotter* than it was yesterday, but differently hot. And, conversely, the *degree*, measured in terms of cubic expansion, is a pure and simply quantity to which there remains attached, in the mind of the layman, a vague idea of a perceptible quality. Modern physics, far from retaining this ambiguous notion, reduces heat to certain atomic *motions*. Where, then, is the intensity? And what is the intensity of a sound or of light but a mathematical relation?

8   Vladimir Ilich Stalin, *Dialectical and Historical Materialism* (New York: International Publishers, [1938] 1940), p. 21.

9 Ibid., pp. 22–3. My emphasis. [Author's note.]

10 Except that they define the milieu more precisely as the mode of material life.

11 The *esprit de sérieux* is one of the two forms of flight from freedom which Sartre identifies in *Being and Nothingness* ([1943] 1956). [Trans.]

12 Stalin, *Dialectical and Historical Materialism*, p. 15.

13 Though Marx did sometimes claim there was. In 1844, he wrote that the antinomy between idealism and materialism had to be overcome. And Henri Lefebvre, commenting on his thought, declares in *Le Matérialisme dialectique* (1962), 'Historical materialism, clearly expressed in *Deutsche Ideologie*, achieves the unity of idealism and materialism prefigured and announced in the "1844 Manuscripts" ' (pp. 53–4). But then why does M. Garaudy, another spokesman for Marxism, write in *Les Lettres françaises*, 'Sartre rejects materialism and yet claims to avoid idealism. The futility of an impossible "third way" here stands revealed . . . '? What confusion there is in these minds!

14 It will perhaps be objected that I have not spoken of the common source of all the transformations of the universe, namely energy; that I have taken my stand on the ground of mechanicalism to evaluate dynamistic materialism. My reply is that energy is not a

directly perceived reality but a concept forged in order to account for certain phenomena; that scientists know it by its effects rather than by its nature and that, at most, they know, as Poincaré said, that 'something remains'. Besides, the little we can say about it is in strict opposition to the requirements of dialectical materialism: its total quantity is conserved; it is transmitted in discrete quantities; it undergoes a constant degradation. This last principle, in particular, is incompatible with the requirements of a dialectic that claims to enrich itself at each new stage. And let us not forget that a body always receives its energy from without (even intra-atomic energy is *received*): it is within the framework of the general principle of inertia that the problems of equivalence of energy can be studied. To make energy the vehicle of the dialectic would be to transform it by violence into *idea*.

15 Stalin, *Dialectical and Historical Materialism*, p. 23.

16 Ibid., pp. 21–2.

17 Here I am summarizing conversations on Trotskyism I have had on many occasions with Communist intellectuals—and not the least significant of them. In every case, they have taken the course I indicate.

18 Ultimately, as we see in the Lysenko affair, the scientist who gave Marxist politics its foundations by providing materialism with its guarantees must now

submit in his research to the exigencies of that politics. This is a vicious circle.

19 Paul Nizan, *The Watchdogs: Philosophers and the Established Order* (New York: Monthly Review Press, 1972).

20 This is what Marx, in the *Theses on Feuerbach* (1924), calls 'practical materialism'. But why materialism?

21 This same ambiguity can be found in the judgements passed by Communists on their opponents. For, after all, materialism should prevent them from making judgements: a bourgeois is merely the product of a rigorous necessity. Yet the entire tone of *L'Humanité* is one of moral indignation.

22 Marx himself lays this out admirably in his *Economical and Philosophical Manuscripts* (1844).

23 This is, once again, Marx's view in 1844, that is to say, before the ill-starred meeting with Engels.

PART FOUR

black orpheus[1]

What were you hoping, when you removed the gags
that stopped up these black mouths? That they would
sing your praises? Did you think, when the heads our
fathers had ground into the dust had raised themselves up again, you would see adoration in their eyes?
Here are black men standing, men looking at us, and
I want you to feel, as I do, the shock of being seen.
For, the white man has, for three thousand years, enjoyed the privilege of seeing without being seen. He
was pure gaze; the light of his eyes drew everything
out of its native shade; the whiteness of his skin was
another gaze, was condensed light. The white man,
white because he was a man, white as day, white as

truth, white as virtue, lit up Creation like a torch, revealed the secret, white essence of other creatures. These black men look at us today and our gaze is driven back into our eyes; black torches light the world in their turn, and our white faces are now just little Chinese lanterns swaying in the wind. A black poet, without even a thought for us, whispers to the woman he loves:

> Naked woman, black woman
> Dressed in your colour which is life . . .
> Naked woman, dark woman!
> Ripe fruit with firm flesh, dark ecstasies
> of black wine.[2]

And our whiteness seems to us a strange pale varnish preventing our skin from breathing, a white undergarment, threadbare at the elbows and knees, beneath which, could we but divest ourselves of it, you would find real human flesh, flesh the colour of dark wine. We thought ourselves essential to the world, the suns of its harvests, the moons of its tides: we are merely beasts among its fauna. Not even beasts:

> These Gentlemen of the City
> These proper Gentlemen

> Who no longer know how to dance
>   by the light of the moon
> Who no longer know how to walk
>   on the flesh of their feet
> Who no longer know how to tell tales
>   around the fire . . .[3]

We, who were once divine-right Europeans, were already feeling our dignity crumbling beneath the gaze of the Americans and Soviets; Europe was already nothing more than a geographical accident, the peninsula Asia juts out into the Atlantic. At least we were hoping to recover a little of our grandeur in the menial eyes of the Africans. But there are no menial eyes any longer: there are wild, free gazes that judge our earth.

> Here is a black man wandering:
>
> to the end of
> the eternity of their
> cop-ridden boulevards . . .[4]

Here, another crying to his brothers:

> Alas! Alas! Spidery Europe moves its fingers
>   and its phalanxes of
> ships . . .[5]

And here,

the insidious silence of this European night . . .[6]
where

. . . there is nothing time does not dishonour.

A Negro writes:

Montparnasse and Paris, Europe and its
endless torments
Will haunt us sometimes like a memory or a
malaise . . .[7]

and suddenly France seems exotic to our own eyes. It
is no more now than a memory, a malaise, a white mist
that lingers in sun-drenched souls, a tormented hinter-
land unpleasant to live in; it has drifted north, it is an-
chored off Kamchatka: it is the sun that is essential,
the sun of the tropics and the sea 'flea-ridden with islands' and the roses of Imanga and the lilies of Iarivo
and the volcanoes of Martinique. Being is black, Being
is fiery, we are accidental and distant, we have to justify *our* ways, our technologies, our half-baked pallor
and our verdigris vegetation. By these calm, corrosive
eyes we are gnawed to the bone:

Listen to the white world
horribly weary from its immense effort

its rebel joints cracking beneath the hard stars,
its blue steel rigidities piercing the mystic flesh
listen to its deceptive victories trumpeting its defeats
listen to the grandiose alibis for its lame stumbling

Pity for our all-knowing, naïve conquerors.[8]

We are *done for.* Our victories, upturned, expose their en-
trails, our secret defeat. If we want to break down this
finitude that imprisons us, we can no longer count on the
privileges of our race, our colour, our technologies: only
by tearing off our white under-garments to attempt simply to be human beings shall we be able to rejoin that totality from which these black eyes exile us.

Yet if these poems shame us, they do so inadver-
tently: they were not written for us. All the colonialists
and their accomplices who open this book will have the
impression that they are reading over someone else's
shoulder, reading letters not addressed to them. It is to
black people that these black people speak and they do so
to talk to them of black people: their poetry is neither
satirical nor imprecatory: it is a *gaining of awareness.* 'So,'
you will say, 'of what interest is it to us other than documentary? We can't enter into it.' I would like to indicate
the route by which we can gain access to this jet-black

world, and show that this poetry, that seems at first racial, is ultimately a song of all for all. In a word, I am speaking here to the whites and I would like to explain to them what black people know already: why it is necessarily through a poetic experience that the black person, in his present situation, must first become aware of himself and, conversely, why black French-language poetry is the only great revolutionary poetry of today.

It is not by chance that the white proletariat seldom employs poetic language to speak of its sufferings, its anger or its pride in itself. I do not believe that the workers are less 'gifted' than our well-heeled young men: 'talent', that efficacious grace, loses all meaning when we claim to ascribe it more to one class than to another. Nor is it the case that the harshness of their labour deprives them of the strength to sing: slaves toiled even harder and we are familiar with slave songs. We have, then, to acknowledge the fact: it is the current circumstances of the class struggle that deter the worker from expressing himself poetically. Being

oppressed by technology, it is a technician he wishes
to become because he knows that technology will be
the instrument of his liberation. If he is to be able
one day to control the management of enterprises, he
knows that only professional, economic, scientific
knowledge will take him there.

Of what poets have dubbed nature he has a deep,
practical knowledge, but it comes to him more
through his hands than his eyes. Nature for him is
Matter, that passive resistance, that inert, insidious ad-
verse force to which he applies the instruments of his
labour; Matter does not sing. At the same time, the
present phase of his struggle calls for continuous,
positive action: political calculation, exact prediction,
discipline, mass organization; dreaming would be treason here. Rationalism, materialism, positivism—these
great themes of his daily battle are the least conducive
to the spontaneous creation of poetic myths. The last
of these myths, the famous 'new dawn', has retreated
before the necessities of the struggle: the most urgent
tasks have to be attended to; a particular position has
to be won, then another; a wage has to be raised, a
solidarity strike or a protest against the war in Indo-

china decided: effectiveness alone counts. And, without a doubt, the oppressed class has first to gain self-awareness. But this awareness is precisely the opposite of a descent into selfhood: it is a question of recognizing, in and through action, the objective situation of the proletariat that can be defined by the circumstances of the production or distribution of goods. United and simplified by an oppression exerted on each and all, and by a common struggle, workers know little of the internal contradictions that nourish the work of art and are detrimental to praxis. For them, to know themselves is to situate themselves in relation to the great forces around them; it is to determine the exact place they occupy within their class and the function they fulfil within the Party. The very language they use is free from the minor slackenings of order, the constant, mild impropriety and transmissive play that create the poetic Word. In their jobs they employ precisely determined technical terms. As for the language of the revolutionary parties, Parain has shown that it is pragmatic: it serves to deliver orders, slogans, information. If it loses rigour, the party falls apart. All this conduces towards the ever more

266

thoroughgoing elimination of the human subject. Poetry, by contrast, has to remain subjective in some way. The proletariat has not had a poetry that was both social and yet drew its sources from subjectivity, a poetry that was social to the very extent that it was subjective, that was founded on a failure of language and yet was as stirring, as widely understood as the most precise of slogans or as the 'Proletarians of all Countries, Unite!' that one finds over the gateways of Soviet Russia. Failing this, the poetry of the future revolution has remained in the hands of well-intentioned young bourgeois who drew their inspiration from their psychological contradictions, from the antinomy between their ideals and their class, from the uncertainty of the old, bourgeois language.

The Negro, like the white worker, is a victim of the capitalist structure of our society; this situation reveals to him his close solidarity, beyond nuances of skin colour, with certain classes of Europeans who are oppressed as he is; it prompts him to plan for a society without privilege, where skin pigmentation will be regarded as a mere accident. But, though oppression is oppression, it comes in different forms, depending on history and geographical conditions: the black man is its victim *as black man*, as colonized native or transported African. And since he is oppressed in, and on account of, his race, it is of his race that he must first gain awareness. He has to force those who, for centuries, have, because he was a Negro, striven in vain to reduce him to the animal state, to recognize him as a human being. Now, no 'way out' offers itself to him here, no deception or 'crossing of the floor': a Jew, who is a white man among white men, can deny that he is Jewish and declare himself a human being among human beings. The Negro cannot deny he is a Negro, nor lay claim to that colourless abstract humanity: he is black. He is, in this way, forced into authenticity: insulted and enslaved, he stands tall, picks up the word 'Negro' that is thrown at him like a stone and proudly, standing up against the white man, claims the name 'black' as his own. The final unity that will bring all the oppressed together in a single struggle must be preceded in the colonies by what I shall term the moment of separation or negativity: this anti-racist racism is the only path that can lead to the abolition of racial differences. How could it be other-

wise? Can blacks count on the assistance of the distant white proletariat, its attention diverted by its own
struggles, before they are united and organized on
their own soil? And does it not, in fact, take a thor-
ough analysis to perceive the identity of deep interests
beneath the manifest difference of conditions? Despite himself, the white worker benefits a little from
colonization: however low his standard of living, it
would be even lower without it. In any event, he is less
cynically exploited than the day-labourer in Dakar or
Saint-Louis. And then the technical installations and
industrialization of the European countries make it
possible to regard socialization measures as immediately applicable there; seen from Senegal or the
Congo, socialism appears, first and foremost, as a
pleasant fancy: for black peasants to discover that it is
the necessary outcome of their immediate, local
demands, they have first to learn to formulate those
demands together and, therefore, to think of themselves as blacks.

But this consciousness differs in nature from the
consciousness Marxism attempts to awaken in the
white worker. The European workers' class conscious-

ness centres on the nature of profit and surplus-value, on the current conditions of the ownership of the instruments of labour—in short, on the objective characteristics of their *situation*. By contrast, since the contempt whites display for blacks—which has no equivalent in the attitude of bourgeois towards the working class—aims to reach into the depths of their hearts, Negroes have to pit a more just view of black *subjectivity* against that contempt; race consciousness is, therefore, centred first on the black soul or, rather, since the term recurs often in this anthology, on a certain quality common to the thoughts and behaviour of Negroes which is termed *negritude.*

Now, to form racial concepts, there are only two ways of operating: either one can convert certain subjective characteristics into something objective or one can attempt to internalize objectively identifiable behaviours. Thus the black man who lays claim to his negritude in a revolutionary movement places himself initially on the terrain of Reflection, either wanting to rediscover in himself certain traits that are objectively observed in African civilizations or hoping to discover the black Essence in the depths of his heart. It is in this way that subjectivity reappears, the subjectivity that is one's own relation to selfhood, the source of all poetry, which the worker has, in self-mutilation, cast off. The black man who calls on his coloured brethren to acquire a consciousness of themselves will try to present them with the exemplary image of their negritude and delve into his soul to grasp it. He wants to be at once a beacon and a mirror; the first revolutionary will be the proclaimer of the black soul, the harbinger who will wrench negritude from himself to hold it out to the world; he will be half-prophet, half-partisan— in short, a poet in the precise sense of the word, *vates*. And black poetry has nothing in common with the outpourings of the heart: it is functional, it meets a need that defines it exactly. Leaf through an anthology of today's white poetry and you will find a hundred diverse subjects depending on the mood and concerns of the poet, his condition and his country. In the anthology I am introducing here, there is only one subject, which all the poets attempt to deal with, more or less successfully. From Haiti to Cayenne, there is a single idea: to *show* the black soul. Negro poetry is evangelical, it announces the good news of negritude regained.

However, this negritude, which they wish to summon up from their uttermost depths, does not fall, of itself, under the soul's gaze: in the soul, nothing is *given*. Those heralding the black soul have attended the white schools, in accordance with that iron law that denies the oppressed any weapon but those they have themselves stolen from their oppressors. It was when it ran up against white culture that their negritude passed from immediate existence to the reflective state. But, as a result, they more or less ceased to live it. By choosing to see what they are, they have become split; they no longer coincide with themselves. And, conversely, it is because they were already exiled from themselves that they have found they have this duty to *show*. They begin, then, with exile. A twofold exile: the exile of their bodies offers a magnificent image of the exile of their hearts. Most of the time they are in Europe, in the cold, amid the grey masses; they dream of Port-au-Prince, of Haiti. But that is not enough: at Port-au-Prince they were already exiled: the slave traders snatched their forefathers from Africa and scattered them. And all the poems in this book (except the ones written in Africa) will offer us the same mystic geography. A hemisphere; right at the bottom, in the first of three concentric circles, stretches the land of exile, colourless Europe; then comes the dazzling circle of the islands and childhood, dancing around Africa; Africa, the last circle, the navel of the world, the hub of all black poetry, dazzling Africa, Africa afire, oily as snake's skin, Africa of fire and rain, torrid and dense, phantom Africa flickering like a flame between being and nothingness, truer than the 'eternal cop-ridden boulevards', but absent, its black rays disintegrative of Europe, yet invisible and beyond reach—Africa, the *imaginary* continent. It is the extraordinary good fortune of black poetry that the concerns of the colonized native find clear, grandiose symbols that have only to be meditated on and endlessly delved into: exile, slavery, the Europe–Africa pair and the great Manichaean division of the world into black and white. This ancestral exile of bodies provides a metaphor for the other exile: the black soul is an Africa from which, amid the cold apartment blocks of white culture and technology, the Negro is exiled. Negritude, present but hidden, haunts him, brushes against him, he brushes against its silky wing, it flutters, stretching out within him as his deepest memory and his highest exigency, as his buried, betrayed childhood and the childhood of his race and the call of the earth, as the seething of the instincts and the indivisible simplicity of Nature, as the pure legacy of his ancestors and as the Morality that should unify his truncated life. But if he turns around to look it in the face, it goes up in smoke; the walls of white culture stand between him and it—*their* science, *their* words, *their* ways:

> Give me back my black dolls, so that I may play
> the naïve games of my instinct with them
> remain in the shadow of its laws
> recover my courage
> my boldness
> feel myself
> a new self from what I was yesterday
> yesterday
> without complexity
> yesterday
> when the hour of uprooting came . . .
>
> they have burgled the space that was mine.[9]

And yet one day the walls of the culture-prison will have to be broken down, one day he will have to return to Africa: in this way, within the *vates* of negri-

tude, the theme of the return to the native country and
the re-descent into the vivid Hades of the black soul
are indissolubly mingled. Involved here is a quest, a systematic stripping-down and an *askesis*, accompanied by
a continuous effort to delve deeper. And I shall term
this poetry 'orphic' because this tireless descent of the
Negro into himself puts me in mind of Orpheus going
to reclaim Eurydice from Pluto. So, by an exceptional
poetic felicity, it is by abandoning himself to trances,
by rolling on the floor like a man possessed and under
attack from himself, by singing his anger, his regret or
his hatreds, by baring his wounds, his life torn between
'civilization' and the old black roots—in short, it is by
displaying the greatest lyricism that the black poet most
surely attains to great collective poetry. In speaking only
of himself, he speaks of all Negroes: it is when he
seems stifled by the serpents of our culture that he
shows himself at his most revolutionary, for then he
undertakes systematically to destroy what he has
learned from Europe and that demolition in spirit symbolizes the great future uprising through which black
people will shatter their chains. A single example will
suffice to throw light on this last remark.

At the same time as they were struggling for their independence, most ethnic minorities in the nineteenth century tried passionately to revive their national languages. To be able to *call* oneself Irish or Hungarian, you have doubtless to belong to a community that enjoys broad economic and political autonomy, but to *be* Irish, you also have to *think* Irish, which means, first and foremost, to think in the Irish language. The specific features of a society correspond exactly to the untranslatable expressions of its language. Now, what is likely dangerously to hold back the effort of black people to throw off our tutelage is the fact that the proclaimers of negritude are forced to frame their gospel *in French*. Scattered to the four corners of the earth by the slave trade, black people have no common language; to encourage the oppressed to unite, they have to resort to the words of the oppressor. It is French that will provide the black bard with the biggest audience among black people, at least within the bounds of French colonization. It is into this gooseflesh language, pale and cold as our skies, which Mallarmé described as, 'the neutral language *par excellence*, since the particular genius of this land demands that all over vivid or riotous colour be toned down'—into this language that is half-dead for them—that Damas, Diop, Laleau and Rabéarivelo will pour the fire from their skies and their hearts. Through it alone can they communicate. Like the scholars of the sixteenth century who could understand each other only in Latin, black people can meet only on the booby-trapped terrain the white man has prepared for them. Among the colonized, the colonialist has arranged to be the eternal mediator; he is there, always there, even when absent—even in the most secret conventicles.

And since words are ideas, when the Negro declares in French that he is rejecting French culture, he takes with one hand what he rejects with the other; he installs the enemy's thinking machine in himself like a mechanical grinder. This would be of no importance, were it not for the fact that this syntax and this vocabulary, crafted in other times and distant climes, to meet other needs and refer to other objects, are unsuitable for providing him with the means for speaking of himself, his concerns and hopes. French language and thought are analytic. What would happen if the black spirit were, above all, a spirit of synthesis? The rather ugly term 'negritude' is one of the only black contributions to our dictionary. But if this 'negritude' is a definable, or at least describable, concept, it must be made up of other more elementary concepts, corresponding to the immediate data of Negro consciousness: where are the words that would enable us to refer to these? How well one understands the lament of the Haitian poet:

This nagging heart, that matches neither
My language nor my costume,
And into which bites, like a clamp,
Borrowed feelings and European
Customs, do you feel this suffering,
This unrivalled despair
At taming, with the words of France,
This heart that came to me from Senegal?[10]

However, it is not true that black people express themselves in a 'foreign' language, since they are taught French from their earliest years and are perfectly at ease in it when they think as technicians, scientists or politicians. We should speak rather of the slight, but constant, gap that separates what they say from what they mean as soon as they speak of themselves. It seems to them that a northern spirit steals their ideas, gently inflects them, so that they mean more or less than they intended; that the white words soak up their thought the way sand soaks up blood. If they suddenly take control of themselves, gather their wits and step back from what is happening, they see the words lying *over against them* in their strangeness, half signs and half things. There is no way they will speak their negritude with precise, effective words that always hit their target. There is no way they will speak their negritude *in prose*. But everyone knows that this sense of failure with regard to language considered as a means of direct expression is at the origin of all poetic experience.

The speaker's reaction to the failure of prose is, in fact, what Bataille calls the holocaust of words. So long as we are able to believe that a pre-established harmony governs the relations between words and Being, we use words without seeing them, with a blind confidence. They are sense-organs, mouths and hands, windows opened on the world. At the first failure, this easy chatter falls away from us; we see the whole system; it is nothing but a broken, upturned machinery, its great arms still waving to *signal* in the void. We judge at a stroke the mad enterprise of naming. We understand that language is, in its essence, prose; and prose, in its essence, failure. Being stands before us as a tower of silence; if we still want to pin it down, it can only be by silence: 'to evoke, in deliberate shade, the silenced object by allusive, ever-indirect words, reducing themselves to an equal silence.'[11] No one has better expressed the idea that poetry is an incantatory attempt to evoke Being in and by the vibratory disappearance of the word. By going further in his verbal impotence, by driving words to distraction, the poet helps us to sense enormous silent densities beyond this self-cancelling hubbub. Since we cannot stop speaking, we have to *make silence with language*. From Mallarmé to the Surrealists, the deep aim of French poetry seems to me to have been this self-destruction of language. The poem is a *camera obscura* in which each word bangs insanely into the next. Colliding in the air, they set each other on fire and fall in flames.

It is within this perspective that we have to situate the efforts of the black evangelists. To the colonialist's ruse, they reply with a similar, but opposite cunning:

since the oppressor is present even in the language they speak, they will speak that language to destroy it. Today's European poet tends to dehumanize words in order to restore them to nature; the black herald, for his part, will *degallicize* them; he will pound them, break down their customary associations, join them together violently.

> With little rain-of-caterpillar steps,
> With little gulp-of-milk steps,
> With little ball-bearing steps
> With little seismic-shock steps
> The yams in the soil are taking great star-gap
>   strides.[12]

He adopts them only when they have disgorged their whiteness, making this language in ruins a solemn and sacred super-language, Poetry. By Poetry alone, the blacks of Antananarivo, Cayenne, Port-au-Prince and Saint-Louis can communicate with each other unwitnessed. And since French lacks terms and concepts for defining negritude, since negritude is silence, to evoke it, they will use, 'allusive, ever-indirect words, reducing themselves to an equal silence'. Short-circuits of language: behind the words falling in flames, we glimpse a large, black, mute idol. It is not, then, simply the intention the Negro has of depicting himself that seems to me poetic. It is also his own way of using the means of expression at his disposal. His situation prompts him to do so: even before he can think of singing, the light of the white words is refracted in him, polarized and altered. Nowhere is this more evident than in the use he makes of the coupled terms 'black/white', which cover both the great cosmic divide between night and day and the human conflict between the native and the colonialist. But it is a hierarchical couple: in delivering it to the Negro, the schoolteacher also delivers a hundred habits of speech that confirm the white man's precedence over the black. The Negro will learn to say, 'playing the white man' to indicate honesty, to speak of 'black looks' and the blackness of a soul or a crime. The moment he opens his mouth, he accuses himself, unless he makes an enormous effort to overturn the hierarchy. And if he overturns it *in French*, he is already being poetic: can you imagine the strange flavour expressions like 'the blackness of innocence' or 'the shades of virtue' would have for us? It is this we savour on each of the pages of this book and, for example, when we read:

Your breasts of black satin,
    curvaceous and gleaming . . .
this white smile
of your eyes
in the shadow of your face
awaken in me, this evening,
the muffled rhythms . . .
that inebriate
our black, naked sisters
over there in the land of Guinea
and stir in me
this evening
Negro twilights heavy with sensual feeling
for
the soul of the black country where
    the ancients sleep
lives and speaks
this evening
in the tremulous strength of your hollow
    loins . . .[13]

Throughout this poem, black is a colour or, rather, a light; its gentle, diffuse radiance dissolves our habitual perceptions: the black country where the ancients sleep is not a dark hell but a land of sun and fire. On the other hand, the superiority of the white over the black isn't merely an expression of the superiority the colonialist claims over the native: at a deeper level, it expresses the adoration of *daylight* and our dread of the night, which is also universal. In this sense, the black writers re-establish this hierarchy they have just overturned. They do not want at all to be poets of the *night*, that is to say, of vain revolt and despair. They are announcing a dawn; they are hailing 'the transparent dawning of a new day'. As a result, the black recovers, at their hand, its sense of gloomy presage. 'Negro, black as misery,' exclaims one of them, and another: 'Deliver me from the night of my blood.'

So the word black turns out to contain both the whole of Evil and the whole of Good; it recovers an almost unsustainable tension between two contradictory classifications: the solar and the racial hierarchies. From this it acquires an extraordinary poetry, like those self-destructive objects produced by Duchamp and the Surrealists; there is a secret blackness of the white, a secret whiteness of the black, a frozen flickering of being and non-being that is nowhere so well expressed perhaps as in this poem by Césaire:

My great wounded statue a stone on its brow
  my great inattentive
pitilessly flecked daylight flesh my great
  night-time flesh flecked with
day [14]

The poet will go even further. He writes of 'Our faces handsome as the true operative power of negation.'[15]

Behind this abstract eloquence redolent of Lautréamont, one glimpses the boldest, most refined effort to give a meaning to black skin and achieve the poetic synthesis of the two faces of night. When David Diop says of the Negro that he is 'black as misery', he presents the black as pure privation of light. But Césaire develops this image and deepens it: the night is no longer absence, it is refusal. Black is not a colour; it is the destruction of that borrowed brightness that comes down to us from the white sun. The Negro revolutionary is negation because he seeks to be a pure stripping-bare: to construct his Truth, he has first to wreck others' truths. Black faces, these patches of night that haunt our days, embody the obscure work of Negativity that patiently gnaws away at concepts. So, by a turnabout that curiously recalls that of the humiliated, insulted Negro when he claims for himself the name of 'dirty nigger', it is the privative aspect of the darkness that establishes its value. Freedom is night-coloured.

Destruction, auto-da-fe of language, magical symbolism, conceptual ambivalence—the whole of modern poetry is here, from the negative standpoint. But this is not an arbitrary game. The situation of black people, their original 'tornness' and the alienation to which a foreign way of thinking subjects them in the name of assimilation oblige them to reconquer their existential unity as Negroes, or, if you prefer, the original purity of their projects, by a progressive *askesis* beyond the universe of discourse. Negritude, like freedom, is both starting point and final end: it is a question of shifting it from the immediate to the mediate, of *thematizing* it. The black person has, then, to die to white culture to be reborn to the black soul, in the same way as the Platonic philosopher dies to his body to be reborn to the truth. This dialectical, mystical return to origins necessarily implies a method. But that method does not present itself as a bundle of rules for the direction of the mind.

It is one with the person applying it; it is the dialectical law of the successive transformations that will bring the Negro to coincide with himself in negritude. It is not, for him, a question of *knowing*, nor of wrenching himself out of himself in ecstasy, but of discovering and, at the same time, becoming what he is.

To this original simplicity of existence there are two convergent paths of access, the one objective, the other subjective. The poets in our anthology at times employ the one and at times the other. Sometimes they use both at once. There is, in fact, an objective negritude that is expressed in the mores, arts, songs and dances of the African peoples. The poet will prescribe for himself, as spiritual exercise, to allow himself to be fascinated by primitive rhythms and let his thought flow into the traditional forms of black poetry. Many of the poems gathered here are called 'tom-toms', because they borrow from the nocturnal drummers a percussive rhythm that is at times spare and regular, at others torrential and bounding. The poetic act is then a dance of the soul; the poet whirls like a dervish until he faints; he has attuned himself to the time of his ancestors, he feels its strange jolting rhythm; it is in this rhythmic flow that he hopes to find himself again. I will say that he is trying to give himself up to possession by the negritude of his people; he hopes the echoes of his tom-tom will awaken the immemorial instincts dormant in him. Leafing through this anthology, you will get the impression that the tom-tom is tending to become a genre of black poetry, as the sonnet and the ode were of ours. Others will take their inspiration, like Rabémananjara, from royal proclamations; yet others will draw on the popular source of the 'hainteny'. The calm centre of this maelstrom of rhythms, songs and cries is, in its naïve majesty, the poetry of Birago Diop: it alone is at rest because it comes straight out of the tales of the *griots* and the oral tradition. Almost all the other attempts have something tense, forced and desperate about them, because they aim to return to folk poetry rather than emanating from it. But, however distant he is from the 'black country where the ancients sleep', the black poet is closer than us to the great age when, as Mallarmé puts it, 'the word creates gods'. It is almost impossible for *our* poets to reconnect with popular tradition: ten centuries of refined poetry sep-

arate them from it and, indeed, the folk inspiration
has dried up; we could at best imitate its simplicity
from the outside. By contrast, black Africans are still
in the great period of mythic fecundity and black fran-
cophone poets do not merely amuse themselves with
these myths as we do with our songs: they allow themselves to be entranced by them, so that at the end of
the incantation, a magnificently evoked negritude
emerges. This is why I call this method of 'objective
poetry' a weaving of spells or magic.

Césaire chose that his homeward journey would
be made walking backwards. Since this Eurydice will
vanish in smoke if the black Orpheus turns around
to look at her, he will descend the royal road of his
soul with his back turned to the far end of the cave;
he will descend beneath words and meanings—'to
think of you, I left all my words at the pawnbro-
kers'[16]—beneath daily behaviour and the plane of
'repetition', beneath even the first reefs of revolt, his
back turned, his eyes closed, so as to be able, at last,
to touch the black water of dreams with his bare feet
and let himself drown in them. Then desire and
dream will rise up roaring like a tidal wave, will make

words dance like driftwood, will throw them, pêle-
mêle, shattered, on to the shore.

> Words transcend themselves, high and low
> > permit of no distraction
> towards a heaven and an earth, the old
> geography is over and done
> > with too . . .
> By contrast, a curiously breathable tiering
> occurs, real, but
> > on one level. On the gaseous level of
> the organism, solid and liquid,
> white and black, day and night.[17]

We recognize the old Surrealist method here (for automatic writing, like mysticism, is a method: learning
and practice must go into it; it must be set going). You
have to plunge beneath the surface crust of reality, of
common sense, of *la raison raisonnante*, to reach the
bottom of the soul and awaken the immemorial powers of desire. Of the desire that makes man a refusal
of everything and a love of everything, a radical negation of natural laws and of the possible, an appeal to
miracles; of the desire which, by its mad cosmic energy, plunges man back into the seething bosom of
nature by affirming his right to dissatisfaction. And

Césaire is not, indeed, the only Negro writer to take this path. Before him, Étienne Lero had founded *Légitime Défense*. 'More than a magazine,' says Senghor, '*Légitime Défense* was a cultural movement. Setting out from the Marxist analysis of the society of the "isles", it discovered the West Indian as the descendant of black African slaves, kept for three centuries in the stultifying condition of proletarian. It asserted that only Surrealism could deliver him from his taboos and express him in his wholeness.'

But, precisely, if we compare Lero to Césaire, we cannot but be struck by their dissimilarities, and the comparison may enable us to measure the abyss that separates white Surrealism from its use by a black revolutionary. Lero was the forerunner. He invented the exploitation of Surrealism as a 'miraculous weapon' and an instrument of research, a kind of radar that you beam out into the uttermost depths. But his poems are schoolboy efforts, they remain strict imitations: they do not 'transcend themselves'. Indeed, they close up on themselves:

The old heads of hair
Stick the bottom of the empty seas to the

291

> branches
> Where your body is but a memory
> Where the spring is doing its nails
> The spiral of your smile cast into the
> distance
> On to the houses we want nothing of . . .[18]

'The spiral of your smile', 'spring . . . doing its nails'—
we recognize here the preciosity and gratuitousness
of the Surrealist image, the eternal practice of throw-
ing a bridge between the two most distant terms, hoping, without too much conviction, that this 'throw of
the dice' will deliver a hidden aspect of being. Neither
in this poem nor in the others do I see Lero demanding the liberation of black people; at best, he calls for
the formal liberation of the imagination. In this
wholly abstract game, no alliance of words even dis-
tantly evokes Africa. Take these poems out of this anthology, conceal the author's name, and I defy anyone,
black or white, not to attribute them to a European
collaborator of *La Révolution Surréaliste* or *Le Minotaure*.
This is because the aim of Surrealism is to recover,
beyond race and condition, beyond class and behind
the incendiary effects of language, a dazzling silent
darkness that is no longer the opposite of anything,

not even daylight, because day and night and all opposites melt and vanish in that darkness. One might
speak, then, of an impassibility, an impersonality of
the Surrealist poem, just as there is an impassibility
and an impersonality of the Parnassian movement.

By contrast, a poem by Césaire flares and whirls
like a rocket; suns burst from it spinning and explod-
ing into new suns; it is a perpetual transcendence. It is
not about joining in the calm unity of opposites, but
of making one of the contraries of the black/white
couple stand up like an erection in its opposition to
the other. The density of these words, thrown into
the air like rocks by a volcano, is negritude defining
itself against Europe and colonization. What Césaire
destroys is not all culture, but white culture. What he
brings out is not the desire for everything, but the revolutionary aspirations of the oppressed Negro. What
he reaches to in the depths of his being is not spirit,
but a certain form of concrete, determinate humanity.
As a result, we can speak here of 'committed', even directed automatic writing—not that thought intervenes, but because the words and images perpetually
express the same torrid obsession. In the depths of

himself, the white Surrealist finds release from tension; in the depths of himself, Césaire finds the stiff inflexibility of protest and resentment. Lero's words are organized flabbily, relaxedly, by a loosening of logical connections, around vague, broad themes. Césaire's words are pressed up against each other and cemented by his furious passion. Between the most daring comparisons, the most distant terms, there runs a secret thread of hatred and hope. Compare, for example, 'the spiral of your smile cast into the distance', which is a product of the free-play of the imagination and an invitation to day-dreaming, with

> and the radium mines buried in the abyss of
>> my innocences
> will leap as grains
> into the birds' feeding trough
> and the stere of stars
> will be the shared name of the firewood
> gathered from the alluvia of the singing
>> seams of night

where the *disjecta membra* of the vocabulary arrange themselves to give us a glimpse of a black *Ars poetica*.

Or read:

> Our faces handsome as the true operative
>   power of negation[19]

and then read:

> and the sea flea-ridden with islands
>   crunching between the fingers of
> the flamethrower roses and my intact body
>   of one thunderstruck.[20]

We have here the transformation scene of the fleas of black destitution jumping around among the hair of the water, 'isles' lying in the light, crunching beneath the fingers of the heavenly de-louser, the rosy-fingered dawn, that dawn of Greek and Mediterranean culture, snatched by a black thief from the sacrosanct Homeric poems, its slave-princess' fingernails suddenly enslaved by a Toussaint Louverture to squash the triumphant parasites of the Negro sea, the dawn that suddenly rebels and metamorphoses, pours out fire like the savage weapon of the whites and, as a flame-thrower, weapon of scientists and torturers, strikes with its white fire the great black Titan, who rises intact and eternal to mount an assault on Europe and Heaven. In Césaire, the great Surrealist tradition comes to its end, assumes its definitive meaning and destroys itself: Surrealism, a European poetic movement, is stolen from the Europeans by a black man who turns it against them and assigns it a strictly defined function. I have stressed above how the entire proletariat closed their minds to this reason-wrecking poetry: in Europe, Surrealism, rejected by those who could have tranfused their blood into it, languishes and withers. But at the very moment it is losing contact with the Revolution, here in the Antilles it is being grafted on to another branch of the universal Revolution; it is blossoming into an enormous dark flower. Césaire's originality lies in his having poured his narrow, powerful concerns as Negro, oppressed individual and militant into the world of the most destructive, freeest, most metaphysical poetry, at a point when Éluard and Aragon were failing to give a political content to their verse. And finally, what is wrenched from Césaire like a cry of pain, love and hatred is negritude-as-object. Here again, he is continuing the Surrealist tradition which wants the poem to *objectify*. Césaire's words do not describe negritude; they do not refer to it; they do not copy it from the outside as a painter does with a model: they *make* it, they compose it before our eyes. From this point on, it is a thing you can observe and come to know. The subjective method he has chosen reunites with the objective method we spoke of above: he thrusts the black soul out of itself at the point when others are trying to internalize it. The final result is the same in both cases. Negritude is a distant tom-tom in the nocturnal streets of Dakar; it is a voodoo cry issuing from a basement window in Haiti, slithering out at street level; it is a Congolese mask, but it is also a poem by Césaire, slobbery, bloody, mucus-filled, writhing in the dust like a severed worm. This double spasm of absorption and excretion beats out the rhythm of the black heart on every page of this collection.

So what, at the present time, is this negritude, the sole concern of these poets, the sole subject of this book? The first answer must be that a white man cannot properly speak of this, since he has no internal experience of it and since European languages lack words that would enable him to describe it. I should, then, let the reader encounter it as he reads these pages and form the idea of it that he sees fit. But this introduction would be incomplete if, having indicated that the quest for the black Holy Grail represented, in its original intention and its methods, the most authentic synthesis of revolutionary aspirations and poetic concern, I did not show that this complex notion is, at its heart, pure Poetry. I shall confine myself, therefore, to examining these poems objectively as a body of testimony and to cataloguing some of their main themes. 'What makes the negritude of a poem,' says Senghor, 'is not so much the theme as the style, the emotional warmth that lends life to the words, that transmutes talk into the Word.' We could not be better warned that negritude is not a state, nor a definite set of vices and virtues, of intellectual and moral qualities, but a certain affective attitude to the world. Since the early part of this century, psychology has given up on its great scholastic distinctions. We no longer believe mental facts are divided into volitions or actions, cognitions or perceptions and blind feelings or   passivities. We know a feeling is a definite way of experiencing our relation to the world around us and includes in it a certain understanding of that universe. It is a tensing of the soul, a choice of oneself and others, a way of going beyond the raw data of experience—in short a *project*, just like an act of will. Negritude, to use Heideggerian language, is the Negro's being-in-the-world.

This is how Césaire puts it:

my negritude is not a stone, its deafness
    hurled against the clamour of
the day
my negritude is not a leukoma of dead liquid
    over the earth's dead eye
my negritude is neither tower nor cathedral
it takes root in the red flesh of the soil
it takes root in the ardent flesh of the sky
it breaks through the opaque prostration
    with its upright patience.[21]

Negritude is depicted in these fine verses far more as act than as disposition. But that act is an inner determination: it is not a question of *taking* the things of this world in one's hands and transforming them; it is a matter of *existing* amid the world. The relation to the universe remains an *appropriation*. But it is not a technical appropriation. For the white man, to possess is to transform. Admittedly, the white worker works with instruments that he does not own. But at least his techniques are his own. If it is true that the major inventions of European industry are attributable to a personnel recruited mainly from the middle classes, at least the crafts of carpenter, joiner and turner still seem to them a genuine heritage, though the direction taken by large-scale capitalist production tends to divest even them of the 'enjoyment of their work'. But it is not enough to say that the black worker works with borrowed instruments; the techniques too are borrowed.

> Césaire calls his black brothers:
>
> Those who have invented neither powder
>   nor compass
> those who could harness neither steam nor
>   electricity
> those who explored neither the seas nor the
>   sky . . .[22]

This lofty claim to non-technicity reverses the situation: what could pass for a failing becomes a positive source of richness. The technical relation to nature discloses it as pure quantity, inertia, externality: it dies. By his lofty refusal to be *homo faber*, the Negro gives it back its life. As if, in the 'man–nature' couple, the passivity of one of the terms necessarily entailed the

300

activity of the other. Actually, negritude is not a passivity, since it 'pierces the flesh of heaven and earth', it is a 'patience' and patience is seen as an active imitation of passivity. The action of the Negro is, first, action on himself. The black man stands and immobilizes himself like a bird-charmer and things come and perch on the branches of this false tree. This is indeed a harnessing of the world, but a magical harnessing through silence and stillness: by acting first on nature, the white man loses *himself* as he loses *it*; by acting first on himself, the Negro aspires to gain nature by gaining himself.

> [They] yield, captivated, to the essence of all
>   things
> ignorant of surfaces but captivated by the
>   motion of all things
> indifferent to conquering, but playing the
>   game of the world
> truly the eldest sons of the world
> porous to all the breathing of the world . . .
> flesh of the world's flesh pulsating with the
>   very motion of the world![23]

On reading these lines, one inevitably thinks of the famous distinction established by Bergson between intellect and intuition. And indeed Césaire calls us 'all-knowing, naïve conquerors'. Of tools the white man knows everything. But the tool scratches the surface of things; it knows nothing of *durée*, of life. Negritude, by contrast, is an understanding through sympathy. The black man's secret is that the sources of his Existence and the roots of Being are identical.

If we wanted to provide a social interpretation of this metaphysics, we would say this was a poetry of farmers pitted against a poetry of engineers. It is not true, in fact, that the black man has no technology: the relation of a human group of whatever kind with the outside world is always technical in one way or another. And conversely, it seems to me Césaire is unfair: Saint-Exupéry's plane, which creases the earth like a tablecloth beneath it, is an instrument of disclosure. But the black man is, first of all, a farmer; agricultural technique is 'upright patience'; it has confidence in life; it waits. To plant is to impregnate the earth; one then must remain still and attentive: 'each atom of silence is the chance of a ripe fruit' (Paul Valéry), every moment brings a hundred times more than the farmer gave, whereas, in the manufactured product, the in-

dustrial worker finds only what he put into it; the man
grows alongside his corn; from one minute to the next
he grows taller and more golden; attentive to this fragile swelling belly, he intervenes only to protect. The
ripe corn is a microcosm because, for it to rise, it took
the contributions of sun, rain and wind; an ear of
wheat is at once the most natural of things and the
most improbable piece of good fortune. Technologies
have contaminated the white farmer, but the black
one remains the great male of the earth, the sperm
of the world. His existence is great vegetal patience;
his work is the repetition year upon year of the sacred
coitus. Creating and fed by what he creates. To plough,
to plant, to eat is to make love with nature. The sexual
pantheism of these poets is doubtless what will first
strike the reader; it is in this respect that they connect
with the phallic rites and dances of black Africans.

> Oho! Congo, lying on your bed of forests,
>   queen of subdued
> Africa. May the phalluses of the hills bear
>   your standard high,
> For you are woman by my head, by my tongue,
> You are woman by my belly[24]

writes Senghor. And:

Now I shall ascend the soft belly of the
dunes and the gleaming
thighs of the day . . .[25]

And Rabéarivelo:

the blood of the earth, the sweat of the stone
and the sperm of the wind.[26]

And Laleau:

Beneath the sky, the conical drum laments
And it is the very soul of the black man
Heavy spasms of rutting man, sticky lover's sobs
Offending against the calm of evening.[27]

We are a long way here from Bergson's chaste, asexual
intuition. It is no longer a question of merely being in
sympathy with life, but of being in love with all its
forms. For the white technician, God is first and foremost an engineer. Jupiter ordains chaos and lays down
laws for it; the Christian God conceives the world by
his understanding and creates it by his will: the relation
of creature to Creator is never a fleshly one, except
for some mystics whom the Church regards with great
suspicion. And even then mystical eroticism has nothing in common with fertility: it is the entirely passive
wait for a sterile penetration. We are *moulded* from clay:

statuettes produced by the *hand* of the divine sculptor.
If the manufactured objects around us could worship
their creators, they would doubtless adore us as we
adore the All-Powerful One. For our black poets, on
the other hand, Being comes out of Nothing like a
male member becoming erect; Creation is an enormous, perpetual giving-birth; the world is flesh and
child of the flesh; on the sea and in the sky, on the
sand-hills, the rocks and in the wind, the Negro redis-
covers the downy softness of human skin; he strokes
himself against the belly of the sand, the thighs of
the sky: he is 'flesh of the flesh of the world'; he is
'porous to all breath', to all pollen; he is by turns the
female of Nature and its male; and when he makes
love with a woman of his race, the sexual act seems to
him the celebration of the Mystery of Being. This
spermatic religion is like a tensing of the soul, balancing two complementary tendencies: the dynamic sense
of being an erect phallus and the more muted, patient,
feminine feeling of being a growing plant. So negritude, at its deepest source, is an androgyny.

    There you are
    standing naked

> clay you are and remember it
> but you are in reality the child of this
>   parturiant shadow
> that sates itself with lunar lactogenic
> then you slowly take the form of a cask
> on this low wall crossed by flower dreams
> and the scent of the resting summer
> feeling, believing that roots are growing at
>   your feet
> and running and twisting like thirsting snakes
> towards some subterranean spring . . .[28]

And Césaire:

> Worn-down mother, leafless mother, you are
>   a poinciana bearing only
> the seed pods. You are a calabash tree, and
>   you are merely a host of
> gourds . . .[29]

This deep unity of plant and sexual symbols is certainly the most original feature of black poetry, particularly in a period when, as Michel Carrouges has shown, most white poets' images tend towards mineralizing the human. Césaire, by contrast, vegetalizes, animalizes sea, sky and stones. More exactly, his poetry is a perpetual coupling of women and men, metamorphosed into animals, plants and stones, with stones, plants and animals metamorphosed into human beings. So the black poet bears witness to the natural Eros; he manifests it and embodies it. If we wanted to find something comparable in European poetry, we would have to go back to Lucretius, the peasant poet who celebrated Venus, the mother-goddess, in the days when Rome was little more than a great agricultural marketplace. In our own day, I can think of hardly anyone but Lawrence with a cosmic sense of sexuality. And, even then, that sense remains, in his case, highly literary.

But though negritude seems, fundamentally, this static outpouring, a union of phallic erection and vegetal growth, this single poetic theme does not encompass it wholly. There is another motif that runs through this anthology like a major artery:

> Those who have invented neither powder
> nor compass...
> Know the furthest recesses of the land of
> suffering.[30]

Against the white man's absurd utilitarian agitation, the black man pits the authenticity he has derived from his suffering. Because it has had the horrible

307

privilege of plumbing the depths of misfortune, the black race is a chosen one. And though these poems are anti-Christian through and through, one might, in this regard, speak of negritude as a Passion: the self-aware black sees himself in his own eyes as the man who has taken the whole of human pain upon himself and suffers for everyone, even the white man.

> Armstrong's trumpet which . . . on the Day
> > of Judgement will speak
> man's pain.
> (Paul Niger)[31]

Let us note right away that this is in no way a resigned suffering. I spoke not so long ago of Bergson and Lucretius; I would be tempted now to quote that great adversary of Christianity, Nietzsche and his 'dionysianism'. Like the dionysian poet, the Negro seeks to penetrate beneath the brilliant fantasies of daylight and, a thousand feet beneath the Apollinian surface, he encounters the inexpiable suffering that is the universal human essence. If we were trying to be systematic, we would say that, insofar as he is sexual sympathy for Life, the black man merges with the whole of Nature and that he proclaims himself Man insofar as he is Passion of rebellious pain. We shall sense the basic unity of this twofold movement if we reflect on the ever-closer relationship psychiatrists are establishing between anxiety and sexual desire. There is but a single proud upsurge, which we can equally well describe as a desire, which plunges its roots into suffering, or a suffering that has driven itself like a sword through a vast cosmic desire. This 'upright patience' evoked by Césaire is, in one single outpouring, vegetal growth, phallic erection and patience against pain: it resides in the very muscles of the Negro; it sustains the black bearer walking a thousand miles up the Niger in overpowering sun with a fifty-pound load balanced on his head. But if we can, in a sense, equate the fertility of nature with a proliferation of woes, in another sense—and this too is dionysian—this fertility, by its exuberance, goes beyond pain, and drowns it in its creative abundance that is poetry, love and dance. To understand this indissoluble unity of suffering, Eros and joy, one has perhaps to have seen the blacks of Harlem dancing frenetically to the rhythm of those 'blues' that are the most sorrowful tunes in the world. It is rhythm, actually, that cements these

309

many aspects of the black soul; it is rhythm that communicates its Nietzschean lightness to those heavy dionysian intuitions; it is rhythm—tom-toms, jazz, the bounding movement of these poems—that represents the temporality of Negro existence. And when a black poet prophesies a better future for his brothers, he does so in the form of a rhythm that depicts to them their deliverance:

> What?
> a rhythm
> a wave in the night through the forests,
>   nothing—or a new soul
> a timbre
> an intonation
> a vigour
> a dilation
> a vibration which, by degrees, flows out in
>   the marrow, contorts in
> its march an old slumbering body, takes it by
>   the waist and whirls
> and turns
> and vibrates in the hands, the loins, the sex,
>   the thighs and the
> vagina . . .[32]

But one must go even further; this fundamental experience of suffering is ambiguous; it is through it that
black consciousness will become historical. Whatever,
in fact, the intolerable iniquity of his present condition, the Negro does not first refer to *it* when he proclaims he has plumbed the depths of human
suffering. He has the horrible advantage of having
known slavery. Among these poets, most of them
born between 1900 and 1918, slavery, abolished half a
century earlier, remains the most vivid of memories:

> My todays each have eyes glowering on my
> yesterdays
> Eyes rolling with rancour, with shame . . .
> I still feel my dazed condition of old
> from
> knotty blows with a rope from bodies
> charred from toe to charred back
> flesh killed by searing brands
> arms broken 'neath the raging whip . . .[33]

writes Damas, the Guyanan poet. And Brière, the
Haitian adds:

> . . . Often like me you feel old aches
> reawaken after the murderous centuries,
> And feel the old wounds bleed in your flesh
> . . .[34]

It was during the centuries of slavery that the Negro drank his fill of the cup of bitterness; and slavery is a past fact that neither our authors nor their fathers knew directly. But it is an enormous nightmare and even the youngest of them do not know whether they have properly awoken from it.[35] From one end of the earth to the other, black people, separated from their colonizers by languages, politics and history, share a collective memory. This comes as no surprise if we remember that, in 1789, French peasants were still subject to fearful panics that went back to the Hundred Years' War. So, when black people look back over their basic experience, it suddenly appears to them in two dimensions: it is both an intuitive grasp of the human condition and the still fresh memory of a historical past. I am thinking here of Pascal who repeated tirelessly that man was an irrational combination of metaphysics and history—inexplicable in his grandeur if he rises above the clay, inexplicable in his misery if he is still as God made him—and that, to understand him, one needed recourse to the irreducible fact of the Fall. It is in this same sense that Césaire calls his race 'the fallen race'. And, in a sense,

I can quite well see how one can compare a black consciousness with a Christian consciousness: the iron law of slavery evokes the law of the Old Testament, which rehearses the consequences of Sin. The abolition of slavery recalls that other historical fact: the Redemption. The suave paternalism of the white man after 1848 and that of the white God after the Passion are similar. Except that the inexpiable Sin the black person discovers in the depths of his memory is not his own, but that of the white man; the first fact of Negro history is, indeed, an original sin, but the black man is its innocent victim. This is why his conception of suffering is radically opposed to white dolorism. If these poems are, for the most part, so violently anti-Christian, this is because the religion of the whites appears even more as a mystification to the eyes of the Negro than it does to the eyes of the European proletariat: it wants him to share the responsibility for a crime of which he is the victim. It wants to persuade him that the abductions, massacres, rapes and tortures that have soaked Africa in blood are a legitimate punishment, are deserved ordeals. You may perhaps say that, on the other hand, it proclaims the

equality of all before God. *Before God*, yes. I read recently in *Esprit* these lines from a correspondent from
Madagascar:

> I am as convinced as you that the soul of a
> Madagascan is of the same value as that of
> a white man . . . Precisely as the soul of a
> child is of the same worth before God as the
> soul of its father. And yet, dear Editor, you
> do not allow your car, if you have one, to be
> driven by your children.

Christianity and colonialism could not be more ele-
gantly reconciled. Against these sophisms, the black
man, by the mere deepening of his memory as one-
time slave, asserts that pain is man's lot and, for all
that, is still undeserved. He rejects with horror the de-
pressive Christian attitude, its morose voluptuousness,
masochistic humility and all the tendentious prompt-
ings to resignation; he lives out the absurd fact of suffering in its purity, injustice and gratuitousness and
discovers in it that truth unknown or concealed by
Christianity: suffering contains its own rejection
within itself; it is, in its essence, refusal to suffer, it is
the shadow side of negativity; it opens on to revolt
and freedom. By so doing, he *historializes himself*, inso-

far as the intuition of pain grants him a collective past
and assigns him a future goal. Just a moment ago he
was pure emergence into the present of immemorial
instincts, pure manifestation of universal, eternal fecundity. Now he calls on his coloured brethren in
quite a different language:

> Black hawker of revolt,
> you have known the paths of the world
> since you were sold in Guinea . . .
> Five centuries have seen you arms in hand
> and you have taught the exploiting races
> the Passion for freedom.[36]

There is already a black Chronicle: first, the golden
age of Africa, then the age of scattering and captivity,
then the awakening of consciousness, the sombre,
heroic days of the great revolts, of Toussaint Louverture and the black heroes, then the fact of the abolition of slavery—'unforgettable metamorphosis', says
Césaire—then the struggle for ultimate liberation.

> You await the next call,
> the inevitable mobilization,
> for your war has known only truces,
> for there is no land where your blood has not
>   flowed,

no language in which your colour has not
　　been insulted.
You smile, Black Boy,
you sing,
you dance,
you dandle the generations
rising every hour,
on the fronts of labour and hardship,
who will rise up tomorrow against the
　　Bastilles,
against the bastions of the future
to write in every tongue,
on the clear pages of every sky,
the declaration of your rights neglected
for more than five centuries . . .[37]

This is a strange, decisive turn: *race* has transmuted
into *historicity*, the black Present explodes and tempo-
ralizes itself, negritude inserts itself with its past and
its future into Universal History. It is no longer a state,
nor even an existential attitude, it is a becoming. The
black contribution to the development of humanity
is no longer a savour, a taste, a rhythm, an authenticity,
a cluster of primitive instincts, but an undertaking that
can be dated, a patient construction, a future. Not so
long ago, it was in the name of ethnic qualities that

the black man claimed his place in the sun; he now bases his right to life on his mission; and that mission, like the proletariat's, comes to him from his historical situation: because he has, more than all others, suffered from capitalist exploitation, he has, more than all others, the sense of revolt and the love of freedom. And because he is the most oppressed, when he works for his own deliverance he strives necessarily for the liberation of all:

> Black messenger of hope
> for you know all the world's songs
> from the songs of the building-sites by the
> Nile
> in times out of mind . . .[38]

But can we still, after this, believe in the inner homogeneity of negritude? And how are we to say what it *is?* At times it is a lost innocence that existed only in a distant past, at times a hope that will be realized only in the radiant city of the future. At times it contracts in a moment of pantheistic fusion with Nature and, at others, it expands to coincide with the whole history of Humanity; it is, at times, an existential attitude and, at others, the objective totality of black-African traditions. Is it something one discovers? Is it something

one creates? After all, there are blacks who 'collaborate'; after all, Senghor, in the notes with which he has
prefaced the work of each poet, seems to distinguish
degrees within negritude. Does the self-appointed
proclaimer of negritude among his coloured brethren
invite them to become ever more black or does he,
rather, by a kind of poetic psychoanalysis, disclose
what they are to them? And is that negritude necessity
or freedom? For the authentic Negro, is it the case
that his behaviour flows from his essence in the same
way as consequences flow from a principle, or is one
a Negro in the same way as a religious believer has the
faith—that is to say, in fear and trembling, in a state of
anxiety, perpetually remorseful at never being sufficiently as one would like to be? Is it a fact or a value?
The object of an empirical intuition or a moral
concept? Is it something achieved by thought? Or
does thinking poison it? Is it only ever authentic when
unthought and immediate? Is it a systematic explanation of the black soul or a Platonic archetype that one
approaches indefinitely without ever attaining it? Is it,
for black people, like our common sense, the most
widely shared thing in the world? Or does it descend

on some like grace and choose its elect? The answer
will no doubt come that it is all these things and many
more besides. And I agree: like all anthropological notions, negritude is a flickering between 'is' and 'ought';
it makes you and you make it: it is pledge and passion
at one and the same time. But there is something
more serious: the Negro, as we have said, creates an
anti-racist racism for himself. He in no way wishes to
dominate the world: he wants the abolition of ethnic
privileges wherever their source; he asserts his solidarity with the oppressed of all hues. The subjective,
existential, ethnic notion of negritude 'goes over', as
a result into the—objective, positive, exact—notion
of proletariat. 'For Césaire,' says Senghor, 'the "white
man" symbolizes capital in the same way as the
"Negro" symbolizes labour. Through the black-
skinned men of his race, he is hymning the struggle
of the world proletariat.' This is easy to say, but less
easy to conceive. And it is doubtless not by chance
that the most ardent high priests of negritude are, at
the same time, Marxist activists. But, even so, the notion of race does not exactly match that of class: the
former is concrete and particular, the latter universal

and abstract; the one derives from what Jaspers calls
understanding, the other from intellection; the former
is the product of a psycho-biological syncretism, the
latter a methodical construction on the basis of experience. In fact, negritude is the weaker up-beat in a
dialectical progression: the theoretical and practical
affirmation of white supremacy is the thesis, the
position of negritude as the antithetical value is the
moment of negativity. But that negative moment is
not sufficient in itself and the blacks who play on it
know this very well; they know its aim is to prepare
the synthesis or realization of the human in a society
without races. Thus negritude is bent upon self-destruction; it is transitional, not final; a means, not an
end. At the moment the black Orpheuses embrace
this Eurydice most tightly, they feel her vanishing in
their arms. A poem by Jacques Roumain, a black
Communist, provides the most moving testimony of
this new ambiguity:

> Africa I have retained a memory of you
>> Africa
> you are in me
> Like the splinter in the wound

> like a tutelary fetish in the centre of the village
> make me the stone in your slingshot
> make my mouth the lips of your wound
> make my knees the broken columns of your
> degradation
> YET
> I want only to be of your race
> workers peasants of the world . . .[39]

With what sadness he holds on, for a moment, to what he has decided to cast off! With what human pride he will shed, for other human beings, his pride as Negro! The person who says both that Africa is in him 'like the splinter in the wound' and that he wants *only* to be one of the universal race of the oppressed, has not thrown off the hold of unhappy consciousness. One step more and negritude will disappear entirely: of what was the mysterious, ancestral seething of black blood, the Negro himself makes a geographical accident, the insubstantial product of universal determinism.

> . . . Is it all these things climate range space
> that create the clan the tribe the nation
> the skin the race and the gods
> our inexorable dissimilarity?

But the poet does not quite have the courage to take over this rationalization of the racial concept: we can see that he confines himself to questioning; beneath his will to union, a bitter regret shows through. A strange path this: hurt and humiliated, black people search in the very depths of themselves to recover their most secret pride, and, when they have at last found it, that pride contests itself: by a supreme act of generosity they abandon it, as Philoctetus abandoned his bow and arrows to Neoptolemus. So Césaire's rebel discovers at the bottom of his heart the secret of his revolts: he is of royal lineage.

> It's true there's something in you that has never been able to bow the knee, an anger, a desire, a sadness, an impatience, in short a contempt, a violence . . . and there's gold not mud in your veins, pride not servitude. A King, you were once a King.

But he immediately wards off this temptation:

> My law is that I run from an unbroken chain
>   to the confluence of fire
> that sends me up in smoke, that purges me
>   and sets me ablaze with
> my prism of amalgamated gold . . . I shall
>   perish, but naked. Intact.[40]

It is perhaps this ultimate nudity of man — wrenching from him the cheap white finery that masked his black breastplate, before undoing, then rejecting, that breastplate itself—it is perhaps this colourless nudity that best symbolizes negritude: for negritude isn't a state; it is pure self-overcoming, it is love. It is at the point where it renounces itself that it finds itself; it is at the moment it agrees to lose that it has won: the coloured man and the coloured man alone can be asked to renounce the pride of his colour. He is the one walking the ridge between past particularism, which he has just ascended, and future universalism that will be the twilight of his negritude; the one who pushes particularism to its limits, to find in it the dawning of the universal. And doubtless the white worker, too, achieves consciousness of his class in order to deny it, since he wishes for the advent of a classless society: but, let me say again, the definition of class is objective; it encapsulates only the conditions of his alienation; whereas the Negro finds race at the bottom of his heart, and it is his heart he has to rip out. So, negritude is dialectical; it is not only, nor is it mainly, the flowering of atavistic instincts; it represents the transcendence of a situation defined by free consciousnesses. The painful and hope-filled myth of Negritude, born of Evil and pregnant with future Good, is as alive as a woman who is born to die and who senses her own death in the richest moments of her life; it is an unstable repose, an explosive fixity, a self-renouncing pride, an absolute that knows itself to be transitory: for at the same time as it announces its birth and its death-throes, it remains the existential attitude that is chosen by free men and lived *absolutely*, drained to the very dregs. Because it is this tension between a nostalgic past, of which the black man is not fully a part, and a future in which it will give way to new values, negritude decks itself in a tragic beauty that finds expression only in poetry. Because it is the living and dialectical unity of so many opposites, because it is a complex resistant to analysis, only the multiple unity of a song and this dazzling beauty of the poem, which Breton terms 'fixed-explosive', can manifest it. Because any attempt to conceptualize its different aspects would necessarily lead to showing its relativity, whereas it is experienced in the absolute by regal consciousnesses and, because the poem is an absolute, it is poetry alone that will enable us to pin down the unconditional aspect of this attitude. Because it is a subjectivity that assumes objective form, negritude must be embodied in a poem, that is to say in an objective subjectivity; because it is an archetype and a value, it will find its most transparent symbol in aesthetic values; because it is a clarion call and a gift, it can be heard and given only through the work of art, which is a call to the freedom of the spectator and absolute generosity. Negritude is the content of the poem, it is the poem as—mysterious and open, indecipherable and allusive—thing in the world; it is the poet himself. We must go even further: negritude, the triumph of narcissism and the suicide of Narcissus, tensing of the soul beyond culture, words and all psychical facts, luminous night of non-knowledge, deliberate choice of the impossible and of what Bataille terms 'torture', intuitive acceptance of the world and its rejection in the name of the 'law of the heart', a twofold contradictory postulate, protesting retraction and expansion of generosity, is, *in its essence, Poetry*. For once at least, the most authentic revolutionary project and the purest poetry emerge from the same source.

And if the sacrifice is one day consummated, what will happen? What will happen if black people, laying aside their negritude in favour of Revolution, no longer wish to see themselves as anything but proletarians? What will happen if they allow themselves to be defined by their objective condition alone; if they force themselves, in order to struggle against white capitalism, to assimilate white technics? Will the source of poetry dry up? Or, in spite of everything, will the great black river colour the sea into which it hurls itself? This does not matter: every age has its own poetry; in every age the circumstances of history elect a nation, a race or a class to take up the torch, creating situations that can be expressed or overcome only through poetry; and sometimes the poetic elan coincides with the revolutionary, and sometimes they diverge. Let us hail, today, the historic opportunity that will enable black people to:

> utter the great Negro cry with such firmness
>   that the world will be
> shaken to its foundations.[41]

Notes

1 First published as the introduction to Léopold Sédar Senghor, *Anthologie de la nouvelle poésie nègre et malgache* (Paris: Presses universitaires de France, 1948). Where the poems cited are extracted from this anthology, I give the references in the form: A, page number.

2 Senghor, 'Femme noire', *Chants d'ombre* (A, 151).

3 Guy Tirolien, 'Prière d'un petit enfant nègre' (A, 87).

4 Léon-G. Damas, 'Un clochard m'a demandé dix sous', *Pigments* (A, 14).

5 Aimé Césaire, 'Et les chiens se taisaient', *Les armes miraculeuses.*

6 Senghor, 'A l'appel de la race de Saba' (A, 152).

7 Jaques Rabémananjara, 'Lyre à sept cordes (Cantate)' (A, 201).

8 Césaire, 'Cahier d'un retour au pays natal' (A, 59).

9 Damas, 'Limbe', *Pigments* (A, 9).

10 Léon Laleau, 'Trahison' (A, 108).

11 Stephen Mallarmé, 'Magie' in *Oeuvres complètes* (Paris: Gallimard, 1945), p. 400.

12 Césaire, 'Tam-tam II', *Les armes miraculeuses*, p. 156.

13 Tirolien, 'L'âme du noir pays' (A, 87).

14 Césaire, 'L'irrémédiable', *Les armes miraculeuses.*

15 Césaire, 'Barbare', *Soleil cou coupé* (A, 56).

16 Césaire, 'Le cristal automatique', *Les armes miraculeuses.*

17 Césaire, 'L'irrémédiable', *Les armes miraculeuses.*

18 Lero, 'Châtaignes aux cils' (A, 53).

19 Césaire, 'Barbare', *Soleil cou coupé* (A, 56).

20 Césaire, 'Soleil serpent', *Les armes miraculeuses* (A, 63).

21 Césaire, 'Cahier d'un retour au pays natal' (A, 58–9). This translation by Clayton Eshleman and Annette Smith, from Aimé Césaire, *The Collected Poetry* (Berkeley: University of California Press, 1983), pp. 67–9.

22 Ibid, p. 67.

23 Ibid, p. 69.

24 Senghor, 'Congo', *Éthiopiques* (A, 168).

25 Senghor, *Chant du printemps* (A, 166).

26 Rabéarivelo, 'Cactus', *Presque–Songes* (A, 189).

27 Laleau, 'Sacrifice' (A, 108).

28 Rabéarivelo, '10', *Traduit de la nuit* (A, 182).

29 Césaire, *Les armes miraculeuses* (A, 73).

30 'Cahier d'un retour au pays natal' (A, 57–8). The second of these lines precedes the first in the published poem.

31 Paul Niger, 'Lune' (A, 104).

32 Niger, 'Je n'aime pas l'Afrique' (A, 100).

33 Damas, 'La complainte du nègre', *Pigments* (A, 10–11).

34 J.-F. Brière, 'Me revoici, Harlem' (A, 122).

35 And, indeed, what is the present condition of the Negro in Cameroon or the Ivory Coast but slavery in the strictest sense of the term?

36 Jacques Roumain, 'Bois-d'Ebène' (A, 114).

37 Brière, 'Black Soul' (A, 128).

38 Roumain, 'Bois-d'Ebène' (A, 114).

39 Roumain, 'Bois-d'Ebène' (A, 116).

40 Césaire, 'Et le chiens se taisaient', *Les armes miraculeuses.*

41 Césaire, *Les armes miraculeuses*, p. 156.

PART FIVE

the quest for the absoluto

Looking at Giacometti's antediluvian face, it does not take long to divine his pride and his desire to place himself at the dawn of the world. Culture he scorns, and he is no believer in Progress either—at least not Progress in the Fine Arts. He sees himself as no more 'advanced' than his adopted contemporaries, the people of Eyzies and Altamira. In those earliest days of nature and humanity, neither ugliness nor beauty existed. Nor taste nor people of taste nor criticism. Everything was still to be done: for the first time it occurred to someone to carve a man from a block of stone.

This was the model, then: the human being. Not being a dictator, a general or an athlete, the human being did not yet have those airs and bedizenments that would attract the sculptors of the future. He was just a long, indistinct silhouette walking across the horizon. But you could already see that his movements were different from the movements of things; they emanated from him like first beginnings and hinted in the air at an ethereal future. They had to be understood in terms of their purposes—to pick a berry or part a briar—not their causes. They could never be isolated or localized. I can separate this swaying branch from a tree, but never one upraised arm or one clenched fist from a human being. A *human being* raises his arm or clenches his fist: the *human being* here is the indissoluble unit and the absolute source of his movements. And he is, besides, a charmer of signs; they catch in his hair, shine in his eyes, dance on his lips, perch on his fingertips. He speaks with the whole of his body: if he runs, he speaks; if he stops, he speaks; and if he falls asleep, his sleep is speech.

And now here is the material: a rock, a mere lump of space. From space, Giacometti has to fashion a human being: he has to inscribe movement in total stillness, unity in infinite multiplicity, the absolute in pure relativity, the future in the eternal present, the loquacity of signs in the stubborn silence of things. The gap between material and model seems unbridgeable, yet that gap exists only because Giacometti has gauged it. I am not sure whether to see him as a man intent on imposing a human seal on space, or a rock dreaming of the human. Or, rather, he is both these things, as well as the mediation between the two.

The sculptor's passion is to transform himself completely into extension, so that, from the depths of that extension, the whole statue of a man can spurt forth. He is possessed by thoughts of stone. On one occasion, he felt a terror of the void; for months he walked to and fro with an abyss at his side; that was space becoming aware within him of its desolate sterility. Another time, it seemed to him that objects, drab and dead, no longer touched the ground; he inhabited a floating universe, knowing in his flesh to the point of torture that there is, in extension, neither height nor depth, nor real contact between things. But at the same time he knew the sculptor's task was to carve from that infinite archipelago the complete form of the only being that can *touch* other beings.

I know no one else so sensitive as he to the magic of faces and gestures. He views them with a passionate desire, as though he were from some other realm. But at times, tiring of the struggle, he has sought to mineralize his fellows: he saw crowds advancing blindly towards him, rolling down the avenues like rocks in an avalanche. So, each of his obsessions remained a piece of work, an experiment, a way of experiencing space.

'He's mad,' they will say. 'Sculptors have been working away for three thousand years—and doing it very well—without such fuss. Why doesn't he apply himself to producing faultless works by tried-and-tested techniques, instead of feigning ignorance of his predecessors?'

The fact is that for three thousand years sculptors have been carving only corpses. Sometimes they are called reclining figures and are placed on tombs; sometimes they are seated on curule chairs or perched on horses. But a dead man on a dead horse does not amount to even half a living creature. They are deceivers all, these stone people of the museum, these rigid, white-eyed figures. The arms pretend to move

but are held up by iron rods, the frozen forms strug
gle to contain an infinite dispersion within themselves.
It is the imagination of the spectator, mystified by a
crude resemblance, that lends movement, warmth and
life here to the eternal deadweight of matter.

So we must start again from scratch. After three
thousand years the task of Giacometti and contemporary sculptors is not to add new works to the galleries,
but to prove that sculpture is possible. To prove it by
sculpting, the way Diogenes, by walking, proved there
was movement. To prove it, as Diogenes did against
the arguments of Parmenides and Zeno. It is necessary
to push to the limits and see what can be done. If the
undertaking should end in failure, it would be impossible, in the best of cases, to decide whether this meant
that the sculptor had failed or sculpture itself; others
would come along, and they would have to begin anew.
Giacometti himself is forever beginning anew. But this
is not an infinite progression; there is a fixed boundary
to be reached, a unique problem to be solved: how to
make a man out of stone without petrifying him. It is
an all-or-nothing quest: if the problem is solved, it
matters little how many statues are made.

'If I only knew how to make one,' says Giacometti, 'I could make thousands . . .'. While the problem remains unsolved, there are no statues at all, but just rough hewings that interest Giacometti only insofar as they bring him closer to his goal. He smashes everything and begins again. From time to time, his friends manage to rescue a head, a young woman or an adolescent, from the massacre. He leaves them to it and goes back to his work. In fifteen years he has not held a single exhibition. He allowed himself to be talked into this one because he has to make a living, but he remains troubled by it. Excusing himself, he wrote: 'It is, above all, because I was goaded by the terror of poverty that these sculptures exist in this state (in bronze and photographed), but I am not quite sure of them. All the same they were more or less what I wanted. Almost.'

What bothers him is that these moving approximations, still halfway between nothingness and being, still in the process of modification, improvement, destruction and renewal, assumed an independent, definitive existence and embarked on a social career far beyond his control. He is going to forget them. The marvellous unity of this life of his is his intransigence in his quest for the absolute.

This persistent, active worker does not like the resistance of stone, which would slow down his movements. He has chosen for himself a weightless material, the most ductile, the most perishable, the most spiritual: plaster. He can barely feel it beneath his fingertips; it is the intangible counterpart of his movements.

What one notices first in his studio are strange spectres made of white blobs, coagulating around long russet strings. His adventures, ideas, desires and dreams are projected for a moment on to his little plaster men; they give them form and pass on, and the form passes with them. Each of these perpetually changing agglomerations seems to be Giacometti's very life transcribed into another language.

Maillol's statues insolently fling their heavy eternity in our faces. But the eternity of stone is synonymous with inertia; it is the present fixed forever. Giacometti never speaks of eternity, never thinks of it. He said a fine thing to me one day about some statues he had just destroyed: 'I was happy with them, but they were made to last only a few hours.' A few hours: like a dawn, a bout of sadness or a mayfly. And it is true that his figures, being designed to perish on the very night of their birth, are the only sculptures I know that retain the extraordinary charm of perishability. Never was material less eternal, more fragile, more nearly human. Giacometti's material, this strange flour with which his studio is powdered, beneath which it is buried, slips under his nails and into the deep wrinkles of his face; it is the dust of space.

But space, even naked space, is still superabundance. Giacometti has a horror of the infinite. Not the Pascalian infinite, the infinitely large. There is another more insidious, secret infinite that runs through his fingers: the infinite of divisibility. 'In space,' says Giacometti, there is too much.' This '*too much*' is the pure and simple coexistence of juxtaposed elements. Most sculptors have fallen into the trap; they have confused profligacy of extension with generosity, they have put too much into their works; they have delighted in the plump contour of a marble haunch; they have spread human action out, fleshed it out, bloated it.

Giacometti knows there is no excess in a living person, because everything is function. He knows space is a cancer of being that gnaws at everything. For him, to sculpt is to trim the fat from space, to compress it so as to wring all externality from it. The attempt may appear hopeless and, on two or three occasions Giacometti has, I believe, been on the verge of despair. If sculpting means cutting up and stitching together again within this incompressible milieu, then sculpture is impossible. 'And yet,' he said, 'if I begin my statue the way they do, at the tip of the nose, it will take me more than an infinity of time to reach the nostril.' That was when he made his discovery.

Take Ganymede on his pedestal. Ask how far he is from me and I will say I don't know what you're talking about. By 'Ganymede', do you mean the stripling carried off by Jupiter's eagle? If so, I'll say there's no *real* relationship of distance between us, for the very good reason that he does not exist. Or are you referring to the block of marble the sculptor has fashioned in the image of the handsome youth? If so, we are dealing with something real, with an existing block of mineral, and we can take measurements.

Painters have long understood all this, because, in paintings, the unreality of the third dimension necessarily entails the unreality of the other two. So the distance from the figures to my eyes is *imaginary*. If I step forward, I move nearer not to them but to the canvas. Even if I put my nose to it, I would still see them twenty paces away since for me they exist definitively at a distance of twenty paces. It follows also that painting escapes the toils of Zeno's paradox; even if I divided the space separating the Virgin's foot from Saint Joseph's into two, and split those two halves again and again to infinity, I would simply be dividing a certain length of the canvas, not the flagstones on which the Virgin and her husband stand.

Sculptors did not recognize these elementary truths because they were working in a three-dimensional space on a real block of marble and, though the product of their art was an imaginary man, they thought they were producing it in real space. This confusion of two spaces has had some odd results. First, when they were sculpting from nature, instead of reproducing what they *saw*—that is to say, a model ten paces away—they shaped in clay that which *was* or, in other words, the model in itself. Since they wanted their statue to reproduce for the spectator ten paces away the impression the model had given them, it seemed logical to make a figure that would be for the spectator what the model had been for them. And that was possible only if the marble was *here* in the same way as the model had been *over there*.

But what does it mean to be *here* and *over there*? Ten paces from her, I form a certain image of this female nude; if I approach and look at her from close up, I no longer recognize her; the craters, crevices, cracks, the rough, black tufts, the greasy streaks, all this lunar orography simply cannot be the smooth fresh skin I was admiring from afar. Is this what the sculptor should imitate? But his task would be endless and, besides, no matter how close he came to her face, it would be possible to get closer.

It follows that the statue will never truly resemble what the model *is* or what the sculptor *sees*. It will be constructed according to certain somewhat contradictory conventions, with some details that are not visible from so far away being shown, on the pretext that they exist, and certain others that exist just as much

343

not being shown, on the pretext that one cannot see them. What does this mean other than that one relies on the eye of the spectator to recompose an acceptable figure? But in that case my relation to Ganymede varies with my position; if near, I will discover details I was unaware of from a distance. And this brings us to the paradox: that I have *real* relations with an illusion or, if you prefer, that my true distance from the block of marble has merged with my imaginary distance from Ganymede.

It follows from this that the properties of true space overlie and mask those of imaginary space. In particular, the real divisibility of the marble destroys the indivisibility of the character represented. Stone triumphs, as does Zeno. Thus, the classical sculptor slides into dogmatism because he believes he can eliminate his own gaze and, without men, sculpt the human nature in man; but, in fact, he does not know what he is making since he does not make what he sees. In seeking the truth, he has found convention. And since, in the end, he shifts the responsibility for breathing life into these inert simulacra on to the visitor, this seeker of the absolute ends up having his work depend on the relativity of the viewpoints from which it is seen. As for the spectator, he takes the imaginary for the real and the real for the imaginary; he searches for the indivisible and everywhere finds divisibility.

By working counter to classicism, Giacometti has restored an imaginary, undivided space to statues. By accepting relativity from the outset, he has found the absolute. This is because he was the first to take it into his head to sculpt human beings as one *sees* them—from a distance. He confers *absolute distance* on his plaster figures just as the painter does on the inhabitants of his canvas. He creates his figure 'ten paces away' or 'twenty paces away' and, whatever you do, that is where it stays. As a result, the figure leaps into unreality, since its relation to you no longer depends on your relation to the block of plaster—art is liberated.

With a classical statue, one must study it or approach it; each moment one grasps new details. The parts become singled out, then parts of the parts and one loses oneself in the quest. You do not approach a Giacometti sculpture. Do not expect this bosom to flesh out as you draw near; it will not change and, as

345

you move towards it, you will have the strange impression of walking on the spot. As for the tips of these breasts, we sense them, divine them, are almost able to see them: one more step, two, and we are still sensing them; another step and everything vanishes. All that remains are puckerings of plaster. These statues can be viewed only from a respectful distance. Yet, everything is there: the whiteness and roundness, the elastic prostration of a fine ripe bosom. Everything except the substance. At twenty paces we feel we can see the wearisome wasteland of adipose tissue. But we cannot: it is suggested, outlined, signified, but not given.

We now know what press Giacometti used to condense space. There is only one: distance. He puts distance within reach. He pushes a distant woman before our eyes—and she keeps her distance even when we touch her with our fingertips. That breast we glimpsed and hoped to see will never spread itself before us; it is merely a hope. These bodies have only as much substance as is required to hold forth a promise. 'Yet that's not possible,' someone might say. 'The same object can't at the same time be viewed close up and from afar.' Hence it is not the same object. It is the block of plaster that is near; it is the imaginary person that is far away. 'Distance should at least, then, effect its contraction in all three dimensions. But it is breadth and depth that are affected; height remains intact.' This is true. But it is also true that human beings possess absolute dimensions for other human beings. If a man walks away from me, he does not seem to grow smaller, but his qualities seem rather to condense while his 'bearing' remains intact. If he draws near to me, he does not grow larger, but his qualities open out.

Yet we must admit that Giacometti's men and women are closer to us in height than in width—as though they were taller than they should be. But Giacometti has elongated them deliberately. We must understand, in fact, that one can neither *learn* to know these figures, which are what they are wholly and immediately, nor observe them. As soon as I see them, I know them. They burst into my visual field like an idea in my mind. Ideas alone have this immediate translucency and are at a stroke what they are. Thus. Giacometti has in his way solved the problem of the unity of the multiple: he has quite simply suppressed multiplicity.

The plaster and the bronze are divisible, but this woman walking has the indivisibility of an idea or a feeling; she has no parts because she yields herself up all at once. It is to give tangible expression to this pure presence, to this gift of self, this instantaneous emergence, that Giacometti resorts to elongation.

The original movement of creation—that timeless, indivisible movement so beautifully figured in the long, gracile legs—runs through these El Greco-like bodies and lifts them heavenward. In them, even more than in one of Praxiteles' athletes, I recognize Man, the first beginning, the absolute source of the act. Giacometti has succeeded in imparting to his material the only truly human unity—unity of action.

This is the kind of Copernican revolution he has tried to introduce into sculpture. Before him, artists thought they were sculpting *being*, and that absolute dissolved into an infinity of appearances. He chose to sculpt *situated* appearance and it turned out that one reached the absolute that way. He gives us men and women *already seen*. But not already seen by himself alone. These figures are already seen in the way that a foreign language we are trying to learn is already spoken. Each of them shows us the human being as he *is seen*, as he is for other human beings, as he emerges in an interhuman milieu—not, as I said earlier for the sake of simplification, ten or twenty paces away, but at a human distance from us. Each imparts to us the truth that man is not there primarily in order subsequently to be seen, but is the being whose essence is to exist for others. When I look at this plaster woman, it is my cool gaze I encounter in her. Hence the pleasant sense of unease which the sight of her occasions. I feel constrained and know neither why nor by whom until I discover that I am constrained to see and constrained by myself.

Giacometti often takes pleasure, in fact, in adding to our perplexity—for example, by putting a distant head on a nearby body, so that we no longer know where to place ourselves or literally how to focus. But even without this these ambiguous images are disconcerting, so much do they clash with our most cherished visual habits. We were accustomed for so long to smooth, mute creatures, made to cure us of the sickness of having a body; these guardian spirits watched over our childhood play and attest, in our parks and gardens, to the fact that the world is risk-free, that nothing ever happens to anyone and hence that nothing has ever happened to them except dying at birth.

Now, to *these* bodies something has happened. Do they come from a concave mirror, a fount of eternal youth or a concentration camp? At first glance, we seem to be dealing with the emaciated martyrs of Buchenwald. But a moment later we have changed our minds: these slim, lissom creatures rise heavenward and we chance on a whole host of Ascensions and Assumptions; they dance, they *are* dances, made of the same rarefied substance as the glorious bodies promised to us by Scripture.[1] And while we are still contemplating this mystical elan, suddenly these emaciated bodies blossom and before us we have merely earthly flowers.

The martyred creature was merely a woman. But she was *all* of a woman—glimpsed, furtively desired, as she moved off and passed by with the comic dignity of those leggy, helpless, fragile girls whom high-heeled mules carry lazily from bed to bathroom with all the tragic horror of the hunted victims of fire or famine; all of a woman—given, rejected, near, remote;

all of a woman, her delicious plumpness haunted by a secret slimness, and her atrocious slimness by a suave plumpness; all of a woman—in danger on the earth and no longer entirely on the earth, who lives and tells us the astounding adventure of flesh, *our* adventure. For, like us, she chanced to be born.

Yet Giacometti is not happy. He could win the game right away, simply by deciding he has won. But he cannot make his mind up to do so. He postpones his decision from hour to hour, from day to day. Sometimes, in the course of a night's work, he is on the point of admitting his victory; by morning, all is shattered. Does he fear the boredom that awaits him on the other side of triumph, that boredom that beset Hegel after he had imprudently rounded off his system? Or perhaps matter is taking its revenge? Perhaps that infinite divisibility he expelled from his work is being endlessly reborn between himself and his goal. The end is in sight: to reach it, he has to do better. And he does so, but now he has to do *a little* better still. And then *just a tiny bit* better. This new Achilles will never catch up with the tortoise. A sculptor has, one way or another, to be the chosen victim of space—if not in his work, then in his life. But above all, between him and us, there is a difference of position. He knows what he was trying to do and we do not; but we know what he has done and he does not. These statues are still more than half embedded in his flesh. He cannot see them. He has barely finished them and he is off dreaming of even thinner, even longer, even lighter women and it is thanks to his work that he conceives the ideal against which he judges that work imperfect. He will never be done with it, merely because a man is always beyond what he does. 'When I finish,' he says, 'I'll write, I'll paint, I'll enjoy myself.' But he will die before he finishes.

Are *we* right or is *he*? To begin with, he is right because, as Da Vinci said, it is not good for an artist to be happy. But we are right too—and right in the last instance. As he lay dying, Kafka asked to have his books burnt and Dostoevsky, in the very last stages of his life, dreamed of writing a sequel to *The Brothers Karamazov*. Both may have died in poor spirits, the former thinking he would slip from the world without even having scratched its surface, the latter feeling he had produced nothing of value. And yet both were winners, whatever they might have thought.

Giacometti is also a winner, and he is well aware of it. In vain does he hang on to his statues like a miser with his pot of gold; in vain does he procrastinate, temporize and find a hundred ruses for stealing more time. People will come into his studio, brush him aside and carry away all his works—even the plaster that covers his floor. He knows this. His hunted air betrays him. He knows that he has won in spite of himself, and that he belongs to us.

Les Temps modernes, January 1948.

calder's mobiles

If it is true that the sculptor is supposed to infuse static matter with movement, then it would be a mistake to associate Calder's art with the sculptor's. Calder does not suggest movement, he captures it. It is not his aim to entomb it forever in bronze or gold, those glorious, stupid materials doomed by their nature to immobility. With cheap, flimsy substances, with little bones or tin or zinc, he makes strange arrangements of stalks and palm leaves, of discs, feathers and petals. They are resonators, traps; they dangle on the end of a string like a spider at the end of its thread, or are piled on a base, lifeless and self-contained in their false sleep. Some errant tremor passes and, caught in their toils, breathes life into them. They channel it and give it fleeting form—a *Mobile* is born.

A Mobile: a little local *fiesta*; an object defined by its movement and non-existent without it; a flower that withers as soon as it comes to a standstill; a pure stream of movement in the same way as there are pure streams of light. Sometimes Calder amuses himself by imitating a new form. He once gave me an iron-winged bird of paradise. It takes only a little warm air to brush against it as it escapes from the window and, with a little click, the bird smoothes its feathers, rises up, spreads its tail, nods its crested head, rolls and pitches and then, as if responding to an unseen signal, slowly turns right around, its wings outspread. But most of the time he imitates nothing, and I know no art less untruthful than his.

Sculpture suggests movement, painting suggests depth or light. Calder suggests nothing. He captures true, living movements and crafts them into something. His mobiles signify nothing, refer to nothing other than themselves. They simply *are*: they are absolutes.

In his mobiles, the 'devil's share' is probably greater than in any other human creation.[2] The forces at work are too numerous and complicated for any human mind, even that of their creator, to be able to foresee all their combinations. For each of them Calder establishes a general fated course of movement, then abandons them to it: time, sun, heat and wind will determine each particular dance. Thus the object is always midway between the servility of the statue and the independence of natural events. Each of its twists and turns is an inspiration of the moment. In it you can discern the theme composed by its maker, but the mobile weaves a thousand variations on it. It is a little hot-jazz tune, unique and ephemeral, like the sky, like the morning. If you missed it, it is lost forever.

Valéry said the sea is always beginning over again. One of Calder's objects is like the sea and equally spellbinding: always beginning over again, always new. A passing glance is not enough; you must live with it, be bewitched by it. Then the imagination revels in these pure, interchanging forms, at once free and rule-governed.

These movements that intend only to please, to enchant our eyes, have nonetheless a profound and, as it were, metaphysical meaning. This is because the mobiles have to have some source of mobility. In the past, Calder drove them with an electric motor. Now he abandons them in the wild: in a garden, by an open window he lets them vibrate in the wind like Aeolian harps. They feed on the air, breathe it and take their life from the indistinct life of the atmosphere. Their mobility is, then, of a very particular kind. Though they are human creations, they never have the precision and efficiency of de Vaucanson's automata. But the charm of the automaton lies in the fact that it handles a fan or a guitar like a human being, yet its hand movements have the blind, implacable rigour of purely mechanical translations. By contrast, Calder's mobiles waver and hesitate. It is as though they make an error, then correct it.

I once saw a beater and gong hanging very high up in his studio. At the slightest draught of air, the beater went after the rotating gong. It would draw back to strike, lash out at the gong and then, like a clumsy hand, miss. And just when you were least expecting it, it would come straight at it and strike it in the middle with a terrible noise. These movements are too artistically contrived to be compared to those, say, of a marble rolling on a rough plane, whose course depends solely on the uneven terrain: the movements of Calder's mobiles have a life of their own.

One day, when I was talking with Calder in his studio, a mobile, which had until then been still, became violently agitated right beside me. I stepped back and thought I had got out of its reach. But suddenly, when the agitation had left it and it seemed lifeless again, its long, majestic tail, which until then had not moved, came to life indolently and almost regretfully, spun in the air and swept past my nose.

These hesitations and resumptions, gropings and fumblings, sudden decisions and, most especially, marvellous swan-like nobility make Calder's mobiles strange creatures, mid-way between matter and life. At times their movements seem to have a purpose and at times they seem to have lost their train of thought along the way and lapsed into a silly swaying. My bird flies, floats, swims like a swan, like a frigate. It is one,

one single bird. And then, suddenly, it breaks apart and all that remain are rods of metal traversed by futile little tremors.

These mobiles, which are neither entirely alive nor wholly mechanical, constantly disconcerting but always returning to their original position, are like aquatic plants swaying in a stream; they are like the petals of the *Mimosa pudica*, the legs of a decerebrate frog or gossamer threads caught in an updraft.

In short, although Calder has not sought to imitate anything—there is no will here, except the will to create scales and harmonies of unknown movements—his mobiles are at once lyrical inventions, technical, almost mathematical combinations and the tangible symbol of Nature, of that great, vague Nature that squanders pollen and suddenly causes a thousand butterflies to take wing, that Nature of which we shall never know whether it is the blind sequence of causes and effects or the timid, endlessly deferred, rumpled and ruffled unfolding of an Idea.

From the catalogue for a Calder exhibition, 1946.

Notes

1 *Corps glorieux.* The reference is to Philippians 3:21. [Trans.]

2 *La part du diable* may be said to be everything that eludes understanding. It is the title of a 1942 work by Denis de Rougement. [Trans.]